"This guide should be required reading for every student in introductory religion and theology courses at the college level. Drawing from significant experience teaching such courses, Rapela Heidt provides helpful and clearly written advice on how to avoid the most common errors of basic writing, punctuation, and citation, as well as step-by-step directions for tackling the research paper. More important, she provides a unique and much-needed resource by walking students through the basics of the Abrahamic faiths and other world religions. Professors who assign this guide will undoubtedly find the papers they grade more gratifying to read."

—M. Therese Lysaught, associate professor of theology,
Marquette University

"Mari Rapela Heidt has produced a much-needed and welcome resource for undergraduate theology majors and minors whose professors require them to follow the writing style presented in the *Chicago Manual of Style*. I would highly recommend this book to my theology students."

—Shawnee M. Daniels-Sykes, SSND, assistant professor
of theology, Mount Mary College

A Guide for
Writing About

Theology
and Religion

Mari Rapela Heidt

ANSELM
ACADEMIC

Created by the publishing team of Anselm Academic.

Cover art royalty free from Shutterstock.com

Printed in the United States of America

7043

ISBN 978-1-59982-003-3

To Larry,
a math guy who knows how to use words,
and
to all of my students
who have ever written about
the "Profit Isaih"

Author Acknowledgments

This book responds to my experiences reading papers written by college students. As such, my first thanks goes to my students, who have inspired this work. I am especially grateful to those motivated to learn about religion and those who worked on making their writing clear and communicative.

Many of my colleagues also contributed to this work. My deep thanks to all who were willing to talk with me about their students' writing, especially my friends in the Religious Studies Department at the University of Dayton.

Another group of colleagues also deserves many thanks. In the fall of 2009, I joined a group of like-minded new professors at the University of Dayton to form the University of Dayton Humanities Faculty Writing Group, the Flying Writers. We have been meeting for some time now to support and encourage one another in our writing endeavors. They influenced most of this manuscript, and my great thanks goes to Heather, Laura, Sam, and others who have encouraged the composition of this work.

My thanks also to my friends and editors at Anselm Academic, especially Jerry Ruff and Brad Harmon, who were willing to see my vision for this book. I thank them for being willing to move this work from random computer files composed for my students to print.

My great thanks also to the librarians and staff of the Waukesha Public Library in Waukesha, Wisconsin, where the final parts of this manuscript were written. Their patience and dedication contributed greatly to the completion of this guide.

Finally, my great thanks to my dear husband, Larry, and our children, Josh, Hannah, and Sarah. Some things cannot be expressed in words, and my feelings toward you are some of those things.

Publisher Acknowledgments

Thank you to the following individuals who reviewed this work in progress:

Marion Grau
Church Divinity School of the Pacific, Graduate Theological Union, Berkeley, California

Peter Huff
Xavier University, Cincinnati, Ohio

John E. McCormick
Newman University, Wichita, Kansas

Contents

Preface

TO STUDENTS

Religion and theology are complex and fascinating subjects that can lead to many new discoveries. Most of the work assigned in theology and religion courses requires some kind of formal writing. This book is intended to help you meet that requirement. Learn the material in this book, and you will be able to complete writing assignments more easily and quickly, and you may see an improvement in your grades.

This guide covers the basics of grammar and punctuation and includes sections on several additional topics that are essential when writing about theology and religion. Topics include drafting thesis statements, avoiding plagiarism, and using inclusive language, as well as various issues associated with writing about a wide range of religions. The guide also includes rules for citing sources and provides numerous sample notes and bibliographic entries. The guide's two appendices provide a checklist for successful paper writing and a list of additional resources. Finally, the index will serve as a handy reference tool for using this guide.

Flag icons in the guide identify particularly important tips and warnings. Single flags, marked with the symbol ▶, indicate tips that warrant special attention. Double flags, marked with the symbol ▶▶, indicate warnings that will help you avoid serious mistakes in your writing.

Keep this book handy as you work on your papers. Use it to help improve your writing and particularly to communicate your ideas about religion and theology clearly and effectively.

TO PROFESSORS

This little book grew out of my experiences with student writing at the college level. Like many professors, I found reading papers frustrating and difficult, not because of the ideas in those papers, but because the ideas were not clearly expressed and the papers themselves were full of grammatical, spelling, punctuation, and usage errors. Many of my students were unaware that they were making multiple mistakes in their papers, primarily because they had never learned the rules of language and formal writing. After many discussions with students about their written work, I began developing computer files about writing to post on the online sites for my courses. These files were essentially crash courses on writing topics, including punctuation, citation, and word usage. These files proved useful: student work improved, especially when students made a determined effort to write better. This book has developed from the files I gave to my students. It is intended, as those first files were, to improve undergraduate writing in religion and theology courses.

The first three chapters of this guide address issues that are particular to the study of religion. Most of these issues revolve around citing texts in various religious traditions, including citing the Bible and the Qur'an, referring to people and rituals properly, and maintaining respect for religious traditions. These chapters are handy for students because they bring together an array of topics—those related most closely to undergraduate study—in one location. This guide leaves discussion of more complex matters to other works. Some of these works are listed in appendix B, Helpful Resources.

Chapter 4, Citing Sources, addresses citation. It explains and illustrates the two different systems of documentation preferred by the University of Chicago Press—the note-bibliography system and author-date system—but gives more attention to the first because that is the system most frequently used in writing about theology and religion. Chapter 4 also notes the difference between a system of documentation and a style. The latter governs the use of mechanics such as punctuation, abbreviations, and parentheses when writing a citation. The sample citations in the author-date system provided in this guide follow the style set forth in *The Chicago Manual of Style* sixteenth edition; however, the citations in a note-bibliography system are illustrated using two different styles: the style set forth in *The Chicago Manual of Style* and a simplified style adapted from the Chicago style. The adaptations in the simplified style were made mainly to make citation more logical and complete while retaining all of the information necessary to meet the goals of citation. In many cases, the only adaptations that have been made are those that streamline typing and make citation less of a chore, such as the elimination of parentheses. Chapter 4's numerous examples of both the Chicago style and the simplified style in the note-bibliography system are clearly distinguished, so students can easily follow one or the other.

I have also given a great deal of thought to the citation of materials from the Internet and have developed some ideas that eliminate a lot of the useless strings of numbers and letters in URLs (web addresses) while still making materials easy to locate. This information is provided in chapter 4.

This guide also includes two brief chapters on grammar and punctuation. These chapters will be a review for some students, but others will need to refer to these chapters repeatedly. You will notice that the chapters are not comprehensive. This is because the guide's material is directed at undergraduates and reflects the typical errors professors see in student writing.

The guide concludes with two appendices—a paper-writing checklist for students and a list of additional resources—and an index that makes the guide a handy reference tool.

I hope that this book will be useful for you and your students and will mitigate some of the frustration that comes from reading papers with significant errors. As noted above, I also hope that this makes writing about religion and theology easier and less frustrating for students, so that they too may find joy and wonder in these subjects.

1

WRITING ABOUT THEOLOGY AND RELIGION

This chapter provides some general information about college-level writing assignments for religion and theology courses. The chapter begins with an overview of formal writing, which includes guidelines for and a discussion of the types of formal writing assignments college students may encounter. Then the chapter provides in-depth information about research papers, the largest writing assignments most college students will complete. The chapter concludes with some discussion of three topics worthy of college students' special attention: avoiding plagiarism, writing with respect for people, and employing sound word usage.

Keep in mind that although this chapter's guidelines are intended to help you navigate writing assignments with greater efficiency and success, for any writing assignment the best source for clarification about expectations, research, sources, and language will be your professor or teaching assistant. They create and grade the assignments and are there to help you learn, so go to them for help with your projects. Librarians and other resource people can offer similar assistance with sources and research. Many schools also have writing centers or writing labs that offer peer-to-peer help with writing.

OVERVIEW OF FORMAL WRITING

Most religion and theology writing assignments call for formal writing. This differs from informal writing, which includes blogs,

Internet postings, journaling, texting, and letters. Formal writing is more objective and less personal than informal writing. It is typically more serious than informal writing in both content and presentation. Many students think formal writing is stuffy and pretentious, using technical terms and stilted language. Although these faults may be common, the goal of formal writing is to communicate with readers, not to bore them. Formal writing need not be dull. The conventions and structures of formal writing serve to help writers communicate their knowledge about and interest in a topic effectively so that readers will find the work informative and satisfying to read.

General Guidelines for Formal Writing

To write formally, follow these general guidelines:

- Approach writing as a conversation with people who are interested in the subject matter. Recognize that the primary audience (usually your professor) knows something about the topic. Present information in a way that builds on the existing knowledge of the audience. This means that you don't have to define every word and explain every principle.
- Be objective and strive to communicate facts and information, not emotions. Aim to persuade through reasoned arguments, not through emotional appeal.
- Use standard English and avoid dialects and regional speech differences (unless quoting from sources that use such language). Remember that your paper is not a speech and using the conventions of spoken English will make for a poor paper. For example, the term *y'all* is common in some areas of the United States and is associated especially with the South. Such colloquialisms should be avoided in papers.
- Use active voice as much as possible. This involves choosing active rather than passive verbs.
- Write complete sentences and express ideas clearly.
- Don't strive to use "important" words or keep a thesaurus by your side to look up long and sophisticated-sounding words.

A common word that communicates well is better than an unfamiliar word that you risk using incorrectly. Clear communication is the goal, not the number of syllables in your words. Do use words that clearly communicate your meaning.

- Limit the use of *I*, *we*, and *you*. The use of *I* and *we* draws attention to your personal perspective, making your presentation subjective when it should be objective. Similarly, the use of *you* makes a direct, personal appeal to the reader, or indicates unjustified assumptions about the reader ("You would be surprised at how many people shop at the mall on Sunday instead of attending church"), which are also out of place in a paper that strives for objectivity. Occasionally no other words will communicate as well as these pronouns, or there may be situations when eliminating these words will make a sentence awkward. If there really is no better alternative, go ahead and use them.

- Limit the use of contractions, like *can't*, *don't*, and *won't*. Spell out most contracted words: *cannot*, *will not*, and *do not*. As above, though, there may be times when eliminating the contraction makes the sentence sound stiff or awkward. Use the contraction if it sounds better, but typically contractions are frowned upon in formal writing.

- Avoid the use of nonstandard abbreviations, emoticons (such as a smiley face), profanity, slang, and other conventions of e-mail and blogging.

- Grammar, spelling, punctuation, and usage are important. Proofread, check your work, and proofread again. Consider reading your writing aloud. This will help you identify poorly constructed sentences. Don't always trust your computer's spelling and grammar checkers. They miss errors and can actually add errors to your papers, such as mistakenly accepting *their* when *there* is required, as in, "He went their not knowing what he would find." Only you can really determine what you are trying to say in your paper. Errors seriously detract from your paper.

- Relax and enjoy writing. When you face challenges, recognize that this is part of learning and contributes to your overall education.

Types of papers

College students studying religion and theology encounter several different types of writing assignments. The purposes of the various types differ, so clarify your assignment before you begin writing. Talk to your professor if you are not sure what is expected.

Research papers typically are the most involved formal writing assignments that undergraduates complete. A research paper presents a thesis or claim and provides an argument that supports the thesis. A thesis statement is not a topic or report subject, such as "The Sacred Texts of Hinduism." A thesis statement articulates a claim or position about some aspect of a topic. For example, you might decide to explore why the Mahabharata, one of Hinduism's two major epics, is so important to many in India. The answers you discover through your research become the basis for your paper's position or thesis. Your thesis may shift as you research and write, so be ready to re-evaluate your thinking as you work. An undergraduate thesis, a long piece of writing that is the capstone to study within a major, is an extended research paper. See the next page for more detailed information about research papers.

An analysis paper asks you to break down a topic or an argument and evaluate each of the parts. The paper then presents this breakdown and your thinking about it. Analysis papers follow the same rules as any other type of formal writing.

A review is essentially an analysis paper focused on a performance, specific piece of writing, film, or piece of music.

A presentation paper is associated with a class presentation. Different professors have different expectations about presentation papers, so read the assignment carefully.

A reflection paper asks students to reflect on a piece of work or a single topic and then summarize their thoughts about it. Journal entries and some other assignments may be considered reflection papers. Although these papers require personal thoughts and ideas without much research, they are also formal writing and should follow all the conventions of formal writing, including proper spelling and punctuation. The major exception is that the frequent use of *I* or *we* is generally acceptable in this kind of paper.

An essay is a short piece of writing that addresses a particular topic. Essays may be written in class or outside of class. Regardless of the topic or the assignment, essays written for class are also formal writing and therefore should follow the guidelines for formal writing.

THE RESEARCH PAPER

The research paper is typically the longest type of writing assigned in a religion and theology course. Working on a research paper provides an opportunity for you to learn a lot about a subject and communicate that knowledge to others clearly and concisely. It is also an opportunity for you to formulate a position or claim about a subject and present information gleaned through research that supports your claim.

Before you begin any research project, clarify the assignment. Be sure you know any parameters set by the professor such as the minimum number of sources you are required to use, the length of the paper in pages or words, and whether the paper will be presented orally in class as well as submitted to the professor in writing. Also find out what method of citation is expected and any other formatting guidelines that your teacher expects you to follow.

Beginning a Research Paper

Work on most research papers begins with the exploration of a general topic. The way to begin a research paper is not simply to jump in and begin writing. Before you can write, you need to do some research to gain the knowledge necessary to determine your paper's purpose and organization. Begin by doing general reading and thinking about the aspects of the topic that raise interesting questions. It is helpful to know what other people have written on the topic and to get some sense of what materials will be available for you to draw on as you write your paper.

After you have done some reading, narrow your topic to something that will be manageable within the limits of a research paper. Some initial ideas are too broad and general to write about in the ten to fifteen pages of a typical research paper. Narrowing your focus will give you a more manageable topic so that you are not overwhelmed and are able to learn about a specific area and easily communicate what you have learned.

For example, suppose that you are taking a course on religion and film. This course requires a research paper of ten to twelve pages on any aspect of religion as it relates to film. You decide that you would like to write about Catholics in the movies. This is an interesting topic with many possible avenues of inquiry. Entire books and numerous articles have been written about this topic. After reading some of this material, you realize that ten pages is not sufficient to cover the entire topic that you had in mind when you began. A narrower focus that appeals to you relates to the roles that the actor Bing Crosby played in movies that were specifically about Catholics, including *Going My Way* and *The Bells of St. Mary's.* This narrower focus will allow you to continue your research without being overwhelmed by the number of sources available for your research.

Formulating a Thesis Statement

A thesis statement articulates the main point or claim that results from research. It is a concise summary of the position that your paper will develop and support. The body of your paper will present information that supports your thesis and will attempt, through sound argument, to persuade the reader that your position is valid or that your interpretation of the information presented is correct.

Students usually form a thesis after evaluating their research when they are able to identify a significant question and make a claim that answers the question. Questions such as who's right?, which side of this issue is more correct?, is this interpretation valid?, is this the best way to analyze this situation?, and what is the relationship between these two areas?, are good starting points for formulating a thesis. The answer to one or more of these questions can become the basis for your paper's thesis.

A clearly articulated thesis statement can provide something of a map for your paper. It lets the reader know what you intend to demonstrate or argue within your paper. The thesis statement should appear early in a paper, usually in the first paragraph or two.

For an example of how to formulate a thesis, let's return to the topic stated above, Bing Crosby's roles in movies about Catholics. From your research, you learn that Bing Crosby was a popular actor who played Catholic characters in several of his movies. You see that your sources suggest that this was important to Catholics in the United States. An initial draft thesis statement might read: Bing Crosby was important to Catholics in the United States. Although it makes a claim, it does not seem to answer a compelling question, so you expand your thinking to consider why Bing Crosby was important to Catholics in the United States. This gives you a new fertile area for research, and you discover that it was the nature of his movie roles that made him an appealing figure. Recognizing this, you modify your original thesis: Bing Crosby was important to Catholics in the United States because of the roles he played in his movies. This has a sharper focus than the first, but you realize that specifying the nature of his roles adds important information about the reasons for his popularity: Bing Crosby was important to Catholics in the United States because his movie roles demonstrated that Catholics were an important part of American society. You decide that this thesis statement articulates a position with significance for your audience that can be developed and supported with evidence gathered through research.

Sources for Research

The best place to begin a research project is with your college or university library. In addition to books, libraries house electronic databases and journals (many of which are not available to the general public), printed journal and folio collections, sophisticated searching software and subject-area databases, and, in some cases, special collections of materials that may help your project. Librarians are knowledgeable about the library collections and how to search them. They can direct you to materials that you might not find on your own.

Books are the most frequently consulted source for research on religious and theological topics. A good place to start is with a specialized religious encyclopedia or dictionary. These sources can provide you with a broad overview of your topic and bibliographical information that can help you identify sources for your research.

As you begin your research, try not to limit your search to religion and theology texts. For example, if you are researching Thich Nhat Hanh, a Vietnamese Zen Buddhist monk blocked from returning to Vietnam in the 1970s, you might consider exploring the political history of Vietnam during the twentieth century to see if it enhances your understanding of him as a religious figure.

Academic journals are also helpful sources for research. Most journals are catalogued in electronic databases, such as ATLA Religion Database and ATLASerials. These databases can be searched by author, title, keyword, or subject. When using a database to search journals, be as specific as possible, because some databases will cite articles only slightly related to your topic if you use imprecise or broad terms. For example, searching for the term *Thich Nhat Hanh* is likely to generate a list of more articles than you can possibly review. Your search of electronic databases will be more fruitful if you can narrow the topic. In the case of Thich Nhat Hanh, if you are interested in the Buddhist meditation center he established in France, you might add the name of the center, *Plum Village*, as a search term. Librarians work with these databases every day, so don't be afraid to ask for help if you are not getting the types of articles you need.

Scholarly books and academic journals contribute greatly to research in religion and theology, but many other materials may be useful, such as prayer books, ritual texts, scriptures, videos, documents from churches or other religious groups, and interviews with religious leaders. In addition, the Internet can provide some useful information. Many churches and religious communities have reliable websites that also provide links to useful related sites. These are fine to use for research, especially if they are combined with other materials, such as books and articles.

Evaluating Sources for Research: General Principles

Learning to evaluate the sources available to you for research is a valuable skill that can translate to areas beyond religious and theological studies. (The same is true of many of the skills, tips, and conventions outlined in this book.) Not all sources of information are reliable, and not all sources that you find will be helpful to your research. Your best guides for assessing sources are professors and librarians, but you can learn to ask and answer the sorts of questions that will help you make determinations on your own. Here are a number of questions to consider when selecting your sources:

- Does the author have the qualifications to write on the topic at hand?
- Does the author's name appear in notes and bibliographies in other works?
- When was the source published? If it is not current, is it still relevant?
- Is the source free from obvious errors and bias?
- Does the author support his or her claims with sufficient evidence?
- If the author offers a unique interpretation or perspective, is the work free of faulty logic?
- If the source is a book, do the book's reviewers affirm the quality of the author's scholarship?
- Does the source address your topic closely enough to be worth the time it will take you to find it and read it?
- Does the source provide enough depth to meet your research needs?

The more of these questions that you can answer in the affirmative, the more you can trust the reliability and usefulness of a source.

As you learn more about your topic, the better you will be at assessing the quality of sources. After you have a sense of what your thesis will be, be careful not to use your thesis as a basis for eliminating sources. If your research yields information that conflicts with your position, pay attention to it. Consider whether the new information challenges you to revise your thesis. Even if it doesn't, this information can be important for your paper. You can describe objections to your thesis and show how these objections do not negate the evidence for your position.

Evaluating Websites

Evaluating information provided via websites requires some special consideration, because the standards for Internet publications are lower than those for print publications. Though Internet sources can provide a vast amount of information, they can also mislead. This is particularly true in the study of religion and theology, subject areas that can generate strong emotion, widely varying interpretations, and positions rooted solely in anecdotal evidence and personal experience.

One way to assess the reliability of websites is to identify their owners or sponsors and then assess both their qualifications and the credentials of the authors who wrote the material that you are considering using for your research. Another assessment strategy is to analyze the nature of a website's material, largely just as you would do for a print source. Are facts substantiated with evidence? Is the information provided accurate? Is the writing free from propaganda and clearly not functioning as an advertisement? Is the material current and does it have a date? Is your view of a web document unrestricted, not a partial view due to limitations in software or a lack of permission to gain full access?

▶ Why not just go to Wikipedia? Wikipedia and other open-source websites like it are not authoritative or reliable sources, although much of the information they present is accurate. Be cautious about these sites, because the entries are the work of numerous people whose motives and authority to write on the subjects at hand are difficult to establish. Because anyone can edit or delete information, the reliability of an entry cannot be counted on from day to day. One person may edit an entry only to find his or her edits reversed the next day or replaced with unsubstantiated claims. Although Wikipedia pages and other websites may provide some inspiration for research and links to some useful sources, they should not be viewed as authoritative sources for research. ◄

SPECIAL TOPICS

This final section of chapter 1 addresses three additional topics worth reviewing before undertaking a writing assignment for a religion or theology course: avoiding plagiarism, writing with respect for people, and employing sound word usage.

Avoiding Plagiarism

Plagiarism is the use of a person's words or ideas in a paper without giving him or her proper credit. Essentially, it is the theft of another person's work. This is a serious offense, and it can lead to significant consequences, such as failing grades, academic probation, suspension, or expulsion.

Plagiarism takes many forms. Copying the words of others into a paper, purchasing an already-written paper, and paying someone else to write a paper for you are all forms of plagiarism. Failing to note quoted material and failing to provide a citation when you use other people's words or ideas is also plagiarism. The proliferation of information in electronic form, through the Internet, online databases, and e-books, has made plagiarism easier. It can be simple to cut and paste information from one electronic source to another. At the same time, the Internet also makes it easier for readers to detect plagiarized material.

Plagiarism can also occur when writers pass off the work of others as their own because of sloppiness or ignorance of citation rules. Sometimes students use quotations or concepts from other people's writing without giving credit because they have taken poor notes and cannot remember where they came across a certain idea. Other times students omit necessary notes thinking that using quotations and footnotes will weaken their papers by making it seem as though they have no original ideas. Sometimes students are unaware that what they are doing is plagiarism, especially if they are paraphrasing an argument from someone else. *Even if it is unintentional, plagiarism is still plagiarism and is still very serious.* This cannot be overemphasized.

To be clear, all of the situations listed above are plagiarism—cutting and pasting, purchasing a paper, not giving credit for a quotation or idea, and even paraphrasing another person's ideas without giving credit for them. It is essential to avoid plagiarism in your papers. The following guidelines will help:

- Leave yourself enough time to write your paper. A lot of dishonesty is the result of desperation when facing a critical due date. If you did not leave yourself enough time to write the paper properly, don't give in to the temptation to purchase or copy a paper. As noted above, plagiarism has serious consequences. Talk to your professor instead. Taking a lower grade is better than being expelled from school.

- Make sure the assignment is clear to you. If you don't understand what you are supposed to do or what kind of paper you are supposed to write, talk to your professor or teaching assistant.

- Don't assume that no one will know that you have purchased a paper or paid someone else to write it or that your professor will not be able to find the source you have cut and pasted into your paper. There will be telltale signs that you did not write the material you are claiming. Professors are experts in their fields and are knowledgeable about the things that are circulating on the Internet about their primary subjects. There are also programs available to professors to assist in finding sources if they suspect plagiarism in a paper. Assuming that no one will know what you have done will only lead to sad consequences.

- Take good notes as you do your research. If you note the sources of your information and quotations as you are preparing to write, citing sources will be easier when you write the paper.

- Understand that footnotes make your papers stronger, not weaker.

- Each time you rely on someone else's work, include a citation. Don't skip any instances, even if they seem redundant.

- Remember that a citation is necessary when you paraphrase another person's idea, not just when you quote the person directly.

- Pay attention to the distinction between someone's original work and common knowledge, which does not require a citation. A fact can be considered common knowledge if it is known by many people or found in many sources. For example, if you write "Brussels, Belgium, is the host city for the 2014 Parliament of Religions," you do not need to provide a citation.

- If you don't understand whether you need to cite something or how to do it, talk to your professor or teaching assistant.

- Make use of writing centers and other writing help offered on your campus.

- Remember that *you* are responsible for all work that you hand in for class. No one else will suffer any consequences for your dishonest or sloppy work. Be sure to review your work to make certain you give the proper credit to others.

Writing with Respect for People

When writing about any religious tradition it is important to maintain respect for people and their beliefs. Learning about religion is likely to expose you to new ideas, some of which may seem odd or strange to you. Religious beliefs can be strongly held and are often deeply integrated into societies. When writing about religion, avoid suggesting that certain ideas or practices are strange. This includes writing about groups that are outside the mainstream of religious practices or beliefs. Respect people by treating their ideas and beliefs with respect. Use words that convey this respect, and avoid labels and stereotypes. Refer to people the way they refer to themselves, and refer to religious groups in a similarly respectful manner, even if you do not agree with their beliefs or understandings.

This section of chapter 1 provides guidance about four aspects of respecting people when writing about religion and theology: using inclusive language, referring to race and ethnicity, using people-first language, and referring to economic classes.

Inclusive Language

Inclusive, gender-neutral language is essential in most settings today. This means avoiding the use of gender-specific nouns to mean all people, as in the phrase, "God's relationship with man." (Try, "God's relationship with humanity" or "God's relationship with people" instead). It is true that the terms *man* and *men* have historically been used as generic nouns that mean all people. This has changed, however, as societies have shifted to different forms of usage to reflect different social norms and changing social understandings. Language has also evolved to reflect these social changes. As a sign of this evolution of language, many publications, both academic and popular, no longer accept exclusive language. Using inclusive language shows respect for human beings in general and for your readers.

In general, avoid gender-specific terms whenever possible. This doesn't just mean avoiding masculine-oriented nouns and pronouns. For example, substituting *she* for *he* and *her* for *his* is just as exclusive as the alternative. Referring to gender is often not necessary, unless a paper is specifically about gender roles or gender exclusion. The best strategy is to rewrite your sentences to eliminate gender references where they are not needed. One easy way to avoid gendered language is to recast your sentences so that the nouns are plural. Pronouns like *they* and *them*, which are inclusive, can then be used in subsequent sentences. Another strategy is to look for neutral alternatives, such as referring to roles instead of people.

▶ Be careful not to mix singulars and plurals in the same sentence; keep subject/object agreement when changing a sentence to incorporate plurals. For example, suppose you use this sentence: "A priest is someone who has dedicated his life to serving God." If you are writing about a church or religion that has both male and female priests, this is not an inclusive sentence. To incorporate inclusive language, you change your sentence to read: "A priest is someone who has dedicated their life to serving God." This sentence, while more inclusive than the first, is incorrect because it mixes a singular subject and verb with a plural pronoun. To be correct, you would have to change all of the elements of the sentence to plurals: "Priests are people who have dedicated their lives to serving God." ◀

Constructions like *he/she*, *him/her*, and the very awkward (and incorrect) *s/he* are unacceptable. This is poor writing. Rewrite your sentences to avoid this. When you do need to indicate *he or she*, spell it out instead of using the slashes.

▶ If you are writing *he or she* in every sentence, consider rewriting several of these sentences in the plural to make writing and reading easier. ◀

Using inclusive language does not require making up words or creating situations where no word is appropriate. It is not necessary to completely eradicate the words *man* and *men* and their compounds. For example, several female members of Congress are "chairmen" of congressional committees. So, be as inclusive as possible but avoid extremes and use common sense in your writing.

Avoid these terms:	Use these instead:
man, men	person, people, humanity
mankind	humankind, humanity, human beings
man-made	manufactured, synthetic
the common man	the average person, ordinary people
any man	anyone
he, him	he or she, her or him, they, them
his	his or her, their

Avoiding stereotyping about gender roles is also a part of inclusive language. Avoid any language that adds gender where it doesn't belong.

Avoid terms like these:	Use these instead:
woman rabbi	rabbi
female doctor	doctor
male aid worker	aid worker, humanitarian aid worker
woman soldier	soldier
male nurse	nurse
woman pastor	pastor

Another aspect of inclusive language is getting rid of diminutives like *–ess* and *–ette* added to the ends of some words to indicate that the person is a woman. Many women find these terms denigrating because they imply that a woman performing the same task as a man is doing something unusual or that her work has less value. Although several of these words in common usage are inoffensive (actress, princess), avoid these types of words except in direct quotations.

Avoid words like these:	Use these instead:
authoress	author
Jewess	Jew
benefactress	benefactor
mayoress	mayor

Race and Ethnicity

Avoid references to race and ethnicity that communicate bias or judgment. For example, avoid using the term *primitive* in reference to an ethnic group's religious beliefs; though some religions have much more complex theologies than others, the word *primitive* suggests that the less complex theology is underdeveloped and implies some sort of evolutionary hierarchy of religious beliefs. It also suggests that the people who hold such beliefs are themselves primitive—that is to say, inferior.

Some theological and religious issues are related to race and ethnicity; in such cases, it is appropriate to make explicit reference to race and ethnicity in your writing. For example, it is appropriate to mention race or ethnicity when writing about the founding of the African Methodist Episcopal Church. Some who write about religion and theology incorporate their experiences of race or ethnicity into their writings. It is appropriate to quote them and to use the same terms that they use in referring to racial or ethnic categories.

If a person's race or ethnicity has no bearing on your work, there is usually no reason to refer to it. When it is necessary to refer to a person's race or ethnicity, use generally accepted terms. If at all possible, determine how people refer to themselves and use those terms in your paper. For example, some people prefer the designation "African-American" while others prefer to be called "black." The same applies to other terms, such as "Native American" versus "American Indian." Remember that your writing should never be offensive.

▶ If you are unsure whether you should use a reference to ethnicity or not, try writing the sentence without that reference. Does your sentence still make sense and convey the same point? If so, you do not need the ethnic reference. ◀

Some religious organizations focus on specific areas of religious faith or practice, such as the Institute for Black Catholic Studies, the Hispanic Evangelism Conference, or the Korean Presbyterian Church in the United States. Be sure to refer to these organizations exactly as they refer to themselves, avoiding shortcuts and slang.

Another aspect of race and ethnicity is seen in the stereotypes that are often associated with particular racial or religious groups. For example, many people use the terms "Arab" and "Muslim" interchangeably. Actually, not all Arabs are Muslims, and not all Muslims are Arabs. Arabic peoples existed before the introduction of Islam, and there are Arabs who are Christian, Jewish, or Muslim, along with others who belong to non-Abrahamic faiths or to no faith at all. Muslims are the followers of the religion of Islam. Muslims can come from any ethnic, racial, or national group and can be found in most countries in the world. The equating of Arabs and Muslims is a stereotype generated by television and the movies. Be aware of such racial and religious stereotyping and avoid it whenever possible.

People-First Language

Some writing about religion and theology requires references to people who face physical challenges. Strive to use people-first language. This is language that emphasizes the person and not his or her disability. For example, use *people with disabilities* not *disabled people*; *people with autism* not *autistic people* or *autistics*. This approach ensures that people are not identified by their disabilities. Using this type of language shows respect for persons and their abilities. (See appendix B, "Helpful Resources," for more resources on people-first language.)

Economic Classes

Many questions within theology and religion address economic issues, such as those that arise in the study of social ethics. Categorizing people by economic class, even when the intention is to write about how these classes can work together, can lead to unintentionally offensive statements or stereotypes. As with other easily misused terms, avoid categorizing people unless the topic of your paper demands it. When you use terms like *the poor*, be clear about what you mean. Use specific numbers and income levels if possible. Avoid any kind of stereotypical implications about people of differing economic classes, for example, that the poor are lazy or that the wealthy have worked harder.

When writing about economic classes around the world, you should also be careful about the implications of your words. Many people object to the classification of countries into "first world" and "third world." Find better and more specific terms to describe the situations of the countries you are writing about. For example, instead of describing the United States as a "first world" country, you might describe it as a wealthy country or an economically developed country. As always, be consistent with the terms you use throughout your paper.

Employing Sound Word Usage

Writing about religion involves a vocabulary of its own, and many of the words used in the study of religion can be easily confused with other words. Some of the most frequently misused words are listed below. Always check a dictionary or your sources if you are unsure about usage.

altar, alter An altar is a table used for worship; to alter something is to change it.

Arab, Muslim These are not interchangeable terms. Not all Arabs are Muslims, and not all Muslims are Arabs.

canon, cannon A canon is a rule or standard; a cannon is a weapon.

censer, sensor, censor A censer is used for incense; a sensor detects something, such as light; to censor something is to examine it and edit out objectionable portions.

cite, site To cite something is to give credit to an original source; a site is a place, either physical or virtual.

girl Use of this term in reference to adults is offensive and indicates a lack of respect for them as people. Use the term *girl* only to refer to children, up until about the age of 14. Adults are women. Teenagers may be "young women" or simply "women."

imam, ayatollah These are terms applied to some leaders in the Muslim faith. Not all Muslims accept these as legitimate terms, so use them carefully.

Israelite, Israeli An Israelite is one of the ancient people of God referred to in the Old Testament; an Israeli is a citizen of the modern nation of Israel. The two terms are not interchangeable.

priest, minister These terms are not interchangeable, and their usage depends on the religious tradition being referenced.

Mass, service, worship Different Christian groups refer to their religious rites and ceremonies in different ways. These terms are not all equivalent. Not all religious rites are Mass, even in the Catholic or Orthodox traditions.

rite, right A rite is a religious ceremony; a right is something that people have a claim to.

satanic, evil Something that is satanic is related to Satan; not all evil is satanic.

tenet, tenant A tenet is a principle or idea; a tenant is someone who rents space from a landlord.

2

WRITING ABOUT RELIGIONS
The Abrahamic Traditions

This chapter discusses some issues that specifically relate to the Abrahamic traditions: Judaism, Christianity, and Islam. These religions are called Abrahamic because they trace their origins back to Abraham, who, it is said, was the first to believe in the one true God, who created all that exists. They are treated together because they have much in common, including many of their beliefs about God and the place of religion in human life. As a result, many of the issues raised in dealing with these traditions are similar.

THE DEITY IN THE ABRAHAMIC TRADITIONS

Jews, Christians, and Muslims confess belief in one God who created the world and reveals God's self to human beings in various ways. Judaism, Christianity, and Islam are monotheistic, that is, they claim that there is only one God. Always write with respect for the deity, even if you are writing about a faith that is not your own or about ideas with which you do not agree. One way of doing this is to capitalize the terms used to refer to or describe God, including the following: Yahweh, Allah, Hashem, Adonai, Heavenly Father, Lord, the Most Benevolent, the Most Merciful, and the Almighty. Christians believe that the one God is triune—three persons in one God. The term *Trinity* and the names of the persons—Father, Son, and Holy Spirit—are always capitalized. All of these are proper nouns, and the rules of grammar and punctuation governing proper nouns apply. Do not capitalize the generic term *god* when not referring directly to the god of a monotheistic faith.

In general, avoid referring to particular terms as God's name. Note that Christians and Muslims do not believe that any of the terms used to refer to God are the actual name of God. Muslims use many different terms for God, including the Most Merciful and the Most Benevolent and other similar terms, although none of these is sufficient to be a name. Allah, which is a common word frequently used in connection with God, is simply an Arabic word that means "God" or "the God"; it is not a name. Christians who speak Arabic use Allah as the term for God. Many Jews understand Yahweh as God's name, referring to Exodus 3:14, where God tells Moses that he is "I am." Other Jews understand this passage as a statement of being, not a name, and believe that God has no name. Much like the Muslim tradition, Christians have many terms that serve as de facto names for God, though it is acknowledged by most that God has no name.

▶ Some traditional Jews (but not all Jews) find it offensive to write out even the word *God*, because the Lord is considered holy and unapproachable. In writings by some Jewish authors, the term *God* is written *G-d*. If you are Jewish or are writing for a Jewish audience, seek your professor's guidance on acceptable ways to refer to God in your writing assignments. ◄

Pronouns

Some Christians have adopted a convention of capitalizing personal pronouns that directly refer to God, using constructions like "praise Him." Most modern English translations of the Bible do not do this, and it is not necessary. However, it is acceptable to many instructors if you are consistent within the paper. The standard practice in academic writing about religion and theology is to use lowercase for all pronouns referring to God.

The use of personal pronouns in English to refer to God requires careful consideration because these pronouns are gendered. If, as many believe, God is neither male nor female, using *he*, *she*, *him*, or *her* in reference to God can mislead and even offend readers. There is no standard practice in English for using pronouns to refer to God.

Seek guidance from your professor on this issue. Some find is acceptable to use the gendered pronouns in relation to God, while others may prefer that students avoid using pronouns to refer to God.

PEOPLE

Revered or Important Persons

Within the Abrahamic traditions, many people are revered for their relationships to God. These people's names are capitalized, but titles like *disciple*, and *prophet* are not. *Saint* is capitalized when used as a title with a name, such as Saint Augustine, but not when used alone or in reference to the members of the LDS Church. *Apostle* is normally not capitalized, but some sources treat it like *saint*. Remember that there are some exceptions to general capitalization rules, so pay attention in your research and be consistent in capitalization throughout the paper.

In Islam, the titles associated with Muhammad are always capitalized, even though the term *prophet* is not generally capitalized in the Jewish and Christian faiths or when referring to others in the Muslim tradition. Be aware that Muslims revere Muhammad as a good and holy man but not as a god or godlike figure.

Examples to illustrate capitalization rules in reference to persons:

the prophet Jeremiah

Moses and the Israelites

Rabbi Gamaliel

the patriarchs

the apostle John

Jesus and his disciples

the Virgin Mary, the Blessed Mother, the Mother of God

the disciples, the women from Galilee

Muhammad, the Prophet, the Messenger

the Muslim people

JUDAISM

People who practice Judaism are called Jews. The nouns *Hebrews*
or *Semites*, which refer to the ancient Israelites, should not be used
to refer to people who practice the Jewish faith today unless they
themselves embrace the term. Use these terms only in the proper
historical context and in direct quotations. If you are unsure about
how to use these terms correctly, ask your professor or teaching
assistant for guidance.

▶▶ The Israelites were the ancient people of God described in
the Tanak (or Tanakh), which Christians refer to as the Old Testament or the Hebrew scriptures. Israelis are the modern citizens of
the nation of Israel. Not all Israelis are Jews, and not all Jews are
Israelis. Do not confuse the two terms. ◀

Leaders in Judaism

Rabbis are leaders and teachers within the Jewish faith. Cantors lead
congregations in worship, and many other people also contribute
to worship. Capitalize these titles only in conjunction with proper
names, if they are referring to a specific person.

Rabbi Bluestein, the rabbi

Cantor Lewis, the cantor

the Hadassah Society

the sisterhood

Unlike Christianity, Judaism has no clergy. Rabbis are learned
men or women who function primarily as teachers and leaders
within the Jewish community. Not all rabbis lead congregations, and
not all congregations are led by a rabbi. Do not use the terms *minister* or *priest* in connection with rabbis. Rabbis may be either male
or female, depending on the division of Judaism to which a given
congregation belongs. Cantors may also be female. Avoid referring to
someone as a *woman rabbi* or *female cantor*. They are simply rabbis or
cantors: the gender reference is unnecessary.

There are several different divisions and groups within Judaism, such as the Hasidim, Reform congregations, and Conservative

temples. These names may differ around the world and from temple to temple or group to group. Learn to recognize the names of these different groups and to use them as they should be used without assigning them qualities that they do not claim. For example, some Conservative Jews (so named because they conserve or save Jewish tradition) are quite politically liberal. Capitalize the names of these groups: Conservative Jews, Reform Jews, Modern Orthodox, Hasidim, Chabad, Orthodox.

▶ Do not confuse the names of groups within Judaism with political parties or groups within the modern state of Israel. For example, United Torah Judaism, Likud, and Kadima are political parties in Israel, not divisions within Judaism. ◄

CHRISTIANITY

Christian is the general term used to refer to people who practice Christianity. The Christian faith has many separate divisions, which are referred to in various ways, including denominations, churches, communions, or groups. Christians, therefore, have more specific identities that reflect their connection to Christianity. Here are some examples: Catholics, Methodists, Lutherans, Presbyterians, Baptists, and Eastern Orthodox.

▶ Members of the Church of Jesus Christ of Latter-Day Saints (LDS) have long been called Mormons. Many members of the church find this to be a derogatory reference made by people who do not respect them or their faith. Other members of the church embrace the term. In your writing, use the terms that seem most common in your sources and be careful to avoid any terms that might give offense to particular groups. Many members of the church use the terms *saints* (without a capital letter) or *LDS members* instead. This is a construction you can consider as long as your writing is clear and you are consistent in usage throughout your paper. ◄

Leaders in Christianity

Christian congregations are usually led by a priest or minister. The terms *priest* and *minister* are not interchangeable, so be sure of the proper term before you use it in your paper. Christians designate the leaders of their congregations in different ways, so be sure you know which terms are proper in context. There are no "priestesses" in the Christian tradition; ordained women are simply priests or ministers, depending on their denominational affiliation. Capitalize proper names and titles but not the terms *minister*, *pastor*, or the like unless they are used in conjunction with proper names. As there are many different groups within Christianity, be sure to use the titles that are proper for that group.

Pastor Hayes, the pastor

Father James Davis, the priest

Reverend Laura Grimes, the reverend

Brother Stephen Jones, Brother Jones

Deacon Nicholas, the deacon

Elder Brown, the elder

When referring to officeholders or leaders of large groups of Christians, be sure to include any suffixes that are a part of the official's name, such as the Roman numerals that follow the names of many popes and some metropolitans. Capitalize the names of the offices when used with a proper name, but use the lowercase otherwise.

Pope John Paul II, the pope

Archbishop Runcie, the Archbishop of Canterbury, the archbishop

Metropolitan Alexis IV, the Metropolitan of Russia, the metropolitan

President Thomas Monson, the president

Religious Communities in Christianity

Religious communities have specific names that should be respected, and the people associated with these communities should be identified as members if they wish to be. Also some general names that are associated with these communities can be used without being considered slang. For example, the men of the Society of Jesus are often referred to as Jesuits. Usually people will add an abbreviation for their community as a suffix after their names. Keep this suffix whenever possible.

Men who belong to religious communities are generally called monks, brothers, or (in some cases) priests; women are called nuns or sisters. Not all monks or brothers are priests, so do not use those terms interchangeably. Use the terms used by the community or the person, and do not imply that monks or brothers are of less importance than priests. The terms *nun* and *sister* mean essentially the same things and can be used interchangeably, according to the preference of the person involved.

> Sister Beverly Lewis, CPPS; Sr. Beverly; the sister
>
> the Sisters of the Infant Jesus
>
> Marianist priest Thomas Hodges; Thomas Hodges, SM; the priest, Thomas
>
> the Sisters of St. Benedict, the Benedictines, the sisters, the nuns
>
> the Cistercians, the monks

Church and church

Some publications use capitalization styles to distinguish between different understandings of the term *church*. For example, in Roman Catholic practice, the "Church" typically refers to the entire people of God and the "church" refers to a specific organization or building. If you are making this distinction in a paper, ask your professor for guidance about using capital and lowercase *c*'s to communicate it. Always capitalize *church* when it is part of a proper name of a place (Church of St. John the Evangelist) or a group (Church of Jesus Christ of Latter-Day Saints). In direct quotations, keep the same capitalization as the original.

ISLAM

People who practice Islam are called Muslims. Although there are many divisions within Islam, it is proper to call any believers Muslims, without reference to the division of Islam to which they belong. If people identify themselves as Sunni Muslims or Shia Muslims, keep those terms. These distinctions, however, are not usually necessary, and many Muslims consider them contrary to a tenet of Islam, that all believers are united.

▶▶ Some older manuscripts use terms like *Muhammadans* or *Saracens* to mean Muslims. These terms are archaic, and many consider them offensive. Use them only in direct quotations, and use those quotations only if you have no other choices. ◀

Leaders in Islam

Two major tenets of Islam are that all Muslims are equal before God and that Muslims need no intermediary to be close to God. Very few leaders speak for large groups of Muslims, and Islam has no clergy that is comparable to any kind of Christian clergy. An imam is a spiritual leader who is somewhat analogous to a rabbi in Judaism. In some mosques, imams may serve as leaders of prayer services or as community leaders, but other mosques rotate such responsibilities among adult men in the community. Some historical figures are also called imams.

In general, refer to people as imams only if they are identified that way in your research. Be aware that not all believers are imams.

Imam Abraham Casey, Imam Abraham, the imam

Caliph and *ayatollah* are somewhat loaded terms in Islam, so be sure to be clear about your meaning when you use these terms. Caliphs were the initial leaders of Islam, who succeeded the Prophet after his death in 632 CE. *Caliph* has also been a political term for men who led various regions. The different divisions of Islam accept different numbers of historical caliphs as legitimate, and some divisions within Islam still seek the return of the caliphates. Use the term *caliph* only in connection with historical events or in writing about modern movements that seek the return of the office of caliph.

An ayatollah is a man who is well versed in Islamic law, culture, ethics, and practice. This office is associated with only some groups in the Shia division of Islam. Other Muslim groups are offended by the idea of such a quasi-ecclesiastical office, so use this term only in reference to specific people who you are certain accept the term. Use it as a title, capitalizing it when linked to a proper name and using the lowercase otherwise.

Ayatollah Khomeini, the ayatollah

TEXTS OF THE ABRAHAMIC TRADITIONS

All of the Abrahamic traditions have sacred texts that are central to their religious understandings and are revered as the words of God. These texts are widely available and many of them will be familiar to you. Familiar or not, they still need to be handled properly within your papers.

Texts of Judaism

The sacred scriptures of the Jewish tradition are a collection of books referred to by Jews as the Hebrew Bible, the Hebrew scriptures, or the Tanak, an abbreviation of the Hebrew titles of the three divisions of the Jewish scriptures: the Law (Torah), the Prophets (Nevi'im), and the Writings (Ketuvim). Christians often refer to these scriptures as the Old Testament, but it is important to recognize that the canon of the Old Testament in Catholic and Orthodox Bibles includes books that were not originally written in Hebrew and do not appear in the Hebrew Bible. The best term to use will depend on which Bible you are citing. Seek your professor's guidance, if necessary, to determine the most appropriate terminology.

▶ The term *Old Testament* is offensive to many Jews, as it might suggest the Hebrew scriptures are "old" in the sense of outdated, less valid, and less valuable than the New Testament. Unless your paper has to do specifically with the Christian interpretation of these scriptures, do not call them the Old Testament. ◀

The Torah is commonly known as the first five books of the Tanak, but the term can also refer to the entire body of teaching surrounding these texts. Be clear what you mean when you use this term. Tanak is always capitalized, as are the titles of other ancient writings. Torah is normally capitalized, but some sources use lowercase when it refers to instruction in general.

To cite the Tanak, see the section on page 40, Citing the Bible and the Tanak.

In addition to the Tanak, many other documents are associated with Judaism, though these are not considered the word of God in the same way as the Tanak. The Pseudepigrapha are texts from the same period as the Tanak that were attributed to important figures but were not actually written by them. Cite these in the same way as the Tanak in your text, but use a footnote to give full publication information for the writing.

The Mishnah and Talmud are other writings you may encounter when writing about the Jewish tradition. These documents have standard names and numbering but still require footnotes with the full publication or translation information when quoted in your papers. Cite documents from the Mishnah by document name, chapter, and paragraph, and the Talmud by folio and side. See the *SBL Handbook of Style* for more information about citing these and other ancient texts.

Texts of Christianity

The sacred scriptures of the Christian tradition consist of a collection of books divided into two parts: the Old Testament and the New Testament. Christians accept the scriptures of Judaism as the revelation of God, usually calling them the Old Testament to contrast with the newer scriptures viewed as sacred only by Christians.

Both the Old Testament and the New Testament have standard names of books and writings and largely standard numbering of chapters and verses. Always capitalize *Old Testament* and *New Testament*. Capitalize *Bible* whenever you are referring to the Christian scriptures. The word *bible* can also be used in lowercase to mean any writing that carries great authority: "*The Chicago Manual of Style* is the bible for many book publishers."

English-language versions of the Christian scriptures are translations from the ancient texts, which were written mainly in Hebrew and Greek. There are numerous versions, including the New American Bible (NAB), the New International Version (NIV), and the New Revised Standard Version (NRSV). Note that there are some differences in the canons of the various Christian denominations. For example, the Roman Catholic and Orthodox canons include several Old Testament books not found in the Protestant canon. Also note that the wording differs from version to version due to differences in the principles of translation used to prepare the texts.

There are few differences in numbering of chapters and verses across versions. Unless you are writing a paper about the differences in translation between versions it is usually not necessary to note which one you are using, though you should use the same version throughout your paper. If you do note the version, use standard abbreviation, usually found somewhere in the beginning or the introduction to the Bible itself.

▶ Many professors prefer one version of the Bible over others. Always use the version you are directed to use. ◀

Citing the Bible and the Tanak

There are two ways to cite passages from the Bible. The first is to refer to the citation directly in the text: "As David said in 2 Samuel 7:18, 'Who am I, Lord, and who are the members of my house, that you have brought me to this point?'" The second way is to give the citation after the quotation, in parentheses: "'Who am I, Lord, and who are the members of my house, that you have brought me to this point?' (2 Samuel 7:18)." The books of the Bible may be abbreviated in notes or parenthetical citations but are usually spelled out in running text. Since the chapters and verses are the same from version to version, you will generally not need a footnote with publication information for the Bible.

▶ When abbreviating books for the Bible, follow one standard style throughout your paper. Mixing styles is sloppy and may suggest to your professor that material has been cut and pasted into your paper. ◀

The parenthetical citation above—2 Samuel 7:18—represents the standard way to refer to the books of the Bible. The first part of a citation is the book from which the quote is taken. In this case, the book is 2 Samuel (this is not chapter 2 of Samuel, but the second book of Samuel). The first number after the name of the book is the chapter. The chapter number is followed by a colon and the number of the verse. So, this citation refers to verse 18 of chapter 7 of 2 Samuel. Some other examples:

Matthew 6:3

James 1:5

Exodus 20:15

When you are referring to a passage that has a range of verses, use a dash between the numbers that indicate the beginning and end of the range:

Matthew 25:31–46

When your passage extends across chapters or even across books, mark the beginning of the passage and the end of the passage, separated by a dash:

John 1:1–2:5

Acts 2:1–3:12

Genesis 12:15–Exodus 20:19

Single numbers used with the title of a biblical book indicate chapters, not verses.

Genesis 1–11 (Genesis chapters 1 through 11)

Revelation 13 (chapter 13 of the book of Revelation)

John 20–21 (John chapters 20 and 21)

▶▶ Never cite the Bible as you would other books, using publication information and page numbers. The numbering and citation system noted above is standard and very clear. ◀

Texts of the Latter-Day Saints (the Mormons)

The Church of Jesus Christ of Latter-day Saints accepts the Book of Mormon and the *Doctrine and Covenants*, along with a book called *The Pearl of Great Price*, as scriptural. No other Christian group accepts these books as valid or as scripture, so do not use them in the study of general Christian beliefs.

Cite *The Pearl of Great Price* as you would any other book, with a full reference in the footnotes. The first reference to *Doctrine and Covenants* should have a footnote similar to this:

[1]All quotations from the *Doctrine and Covenants* are taken from Joseph Smith, *Book of Doctrine and Covenants, Carefully Selected from the Revelations of God and Given in Order of Their Dates* (Independence, MO: Herald Publishing House, 2000).

See chapter 4 for complete information on using footnotes.

Subsequent references can be handled with parenthetical citations in the running texts. *Doctrine and Covenants* is divided into 138 sections, and the verses in each section are numbered. Mormon scholars cite the text by abbreviating the title and noting the section and verse numbers:

D&C 88:118.

The Book of Mormon is arranged in numbered chapters and verses similar to the Bible. In your text, cite the Book of Mormon in the same format as you would the Bible, noting the book, chapter, and verse. As with the Bible, no publication information is necessary. For example:

Nephi 1:6

Mormon 8:3

Texts of Islam

The Qur'an is the holy book of Islam. Muslims believe that it is the actual word of God, given as a gift to the people. Muhammad received or recited the Qur'an, but he did not write it. The language of the Qur'an is Arabic, although translations exist in almost every language.

Qur'an is the preferred spelling for most Muslims in the West. It can also be written as Quran, without the apostrophe. The term Koran is common but does not reflect the true pronunciation in Arabic and is as incorrect as calling Mumbai, India, by its former name, Bombay.

▶ Avoid writing that the Qur'an is "the Bible of Islam." Comparison with the Bible suggests that the Qur'an is a collection of books, which is not the case. ◄

The Qur'an is divided into chapters (*suras*) and verses (*ayut*), much like the Bible, and should be cited using the number of the chapter and the verse, separated by a colon in the same way that the chapters and verses of the Christian Bible are cited. For example: "There is no compulsion in matters of religion" (2:256). Chapters of the Qur'an also have names that can be referred to informally in the text, with the chapter and verse noted in parentheses, as in this example:

> Crucifixion is referred to in the Qur'an in the chapter "The Women" (4:154–59).

Unlike the Bible, the Qur'an requires a footnote with translation and publication information. There are many English translations of the Qur'an, but none of these translations can be considered standard. The first time you use a reference to the Qur'an, add a footnote that gives the publication information and translator. References after the first one will not need additional footnotes. (See chapter 4 for more on how to use footnotes.) Do not use page numbers for citations in the Qur'an.

▶▶ Many word processing programs can render text in Arabic. Resist the temptation to copy the verses of the Qur'an in Arabic into your papers, however beautiful they may look. Muslims consider the verses in Arabic to be the very words of God; any paper that they are written on becomes a sacred object, like the Qur'an itself. Copying them into a paper for a class would be considered quite offensive. ◄

There are other important writings in Islam, but none are considered scriptural. The *sunnah* of the Prophet, which generally refers to the sayings and life of Muhammad, and the hadith, commentaries on life and ethics, require footnotes and full publication information, along with page numbers.

RELIGIOUS SERVICES AND RITES

Services and Rites of Judaism

Worship services and rites are important to the Jewish faith, to varying degrees within the different Jewish groups. Many Jewish ceremonies and rites are conducted in the home, but others take place in a synagogue or temple. When giving the title of a congregation, pay attention to the punctuation and capitalization used by the group itself. Most temple or synagogue names are transliterations from Hebrew and can be spelled in English in different ways. Also, Jewish houses of worship can be known as synagogues, temples, houses, or congregations. Use the name the group uses for itself.

> Congregation Emanu-el
>
> Temple Israel
>
> Chabad House
>
> Temple Abraham

Jewish worship is generally referred to as a service, never Mass. Not all services are presided over by a rabbi. In many Jewish services, any adult male can lead the service. In some groups within Judaism, adult women may preside as well.

Use lowercase to signify the names of services or rituals and uppercase (capitals) for the names of holidays. Know the difference between the two. As always, there are some exceptions, so pay attention in your reading and research.

Examples:

> The Sabbath begins every Friday night.
>
> Joshua's bar mitzvah will be held at the temple.
>
> The bris is open to all members of the congregation.
>
> The Seder is a meal celebrating the Passover.

Services and Rites of Christianity

There are a variety of types of Christian worship services. Christians worship in various settings including churches, homes, and makeshift worship spaces such as gymnasiums. Use the name of a congregation or community that the group itself uses, retaining the same punctuation and capitalization. For example:

Church of the Transfiguration

Congregation of St. Mary Magdalen

Maranatha Church of God in Christ

Church of Acts

Westfield Bible Church

The central celebration of Catholics, Anglicans, and some Orthodox is called Mass, which is always capitalized: funeral Mass, Easter Mass. If applicable, make the distinction between High Mass and Low Mass in the Anglican tradition, capitalizing High and Low. Other Catholic, Orthodox, or Anglican liturgies or worship services, such as prayer services, funerals, matins (or morning prayer), and sacraments are usually written in lowercase.

Protestant denominations have services, worship, or worship services. These are written in lowercase. Quakers have meetings, as do some groups of the Amish. These are a part of the rituals of the faith and unlike the meetings of other groups.

While the names of sacraments are usually lowercase, holidays are uppercase: baptism, confirmation, and marriage, but Easter, Christmas, and the Feast of the Transfiguration. Eucharist, though a sacrament, is capitalized because it refers to the Mass. Seasons or periods within the Christian year are also capitalized: Advent, Lent. Be aware that these are general guidelines and that you may see widely varying capitalization practices. For example, documents written by church authorities sometimes employ different rules for referring to and capitalizing sacraments and rites. For your papers, follow the guidelines laid out here unless otherwise directed by your professor.

Services and Rites of Islam

In the Muslim tradition, worship is intended to be a constant part of each day, but Muslims also gather for worship services, which can be held in a mosque, a home, or other places. When writing the name of a mosque, use the same punctuation and capitalization the mosque itself uses. Be aware that some Muslim community centers are also mosques and that *masjid* is an Arabic word that means mosque. For example:

> Masjid Sultan Muhammad
> Islamic Center of Dayton
> Masjid al-Haqq
> Islamic Community Center

All Muslim services can be referred to as worship services. The names of holidays and periods or seasons within the Islamic year are capitalized. For example:

> Eid al-Fitr
> Ramadan
> Ashura

SPECIAL QUESTIONS RELATED TO THE ABRAHAMIC TRADITIONS

Prayers and Prayer Books

Capitalize the titles of common prayers and prayer books in any of the traditions. The titles of creeds are also capitalized. For example:

> the Book of Common Prayer
> the Lord's Prayer
> Kaddish
> the Shema
> Salat al-Fajr
> the Nicene Creed

The Councils and Synods of the Christian Tradition

The titles of councils and major synods in the Christian tradition are always capitalized. Short versions of titles are acceptable on the second reference.

the Second Vatican Council, Vatican II

the Council of Chalcedon, Chalcedon

the General Convention, the Convention

Important Documents in the Catholic Tradition

Popes, other Vatican officials, the various congregations and committees of the Catholic Church, and local conferences of bishops such as the United States Conference of Catholic Bishops have published numerous documents intended for Catholics as well as other Christians and adherents of other religions. There are fairly standard ways of citing these documents.

Encyclicals, Apostolic Letters, Motu Propria, and Similar Communications

These documents are traditionally named by the first Latin phrase of the document, and you should refer to the document by this phrase throughout your paper. For footnotes or endnotes, follow these examples.

First reference:

[1]Pope John Paul II, *Evangelium Vitae*, March 25, 1995, no. 26.

[1]Pope Paul VI, *Octogesima Adveniens*, May 14, 1971, no. 6.

Second and subsequent references:

[2]*Evangelium Vitae*, no. 26.

or:

[2]*EV*, no. 26.

[2]*Octogesima Adveniens*, no. 6.

or:

[2]*OA*, no. 6.

In the example above, the final number is the paragraph number in which one's quotation or material is found. Also note that the titles of papal documents like this are always italicized. Always translate the pope's name into English; do not use the Latin that is the traditional signature of the pope. Thus, "Pope John Paul II," *not* "Ioannes Paulus PP. II." If you have trouble with the Latin names, first look at the beginning of the document. The translated name of the author will often be given at the beginning, with the traditional Latin at the end. Otherwise, consult your sources or a good religious encyclopedia for information on the author.

Other Types of Pronouncements, Documents, and Speeches

First reference:

> [1]Pope Paul VI, "Message for the Celebration of the Day of Peace," December 8, 1971.

Second and subsequent references:

> [2]Pope Paul VI, "Message."

Use line or paragraph numbers if available. Always use the English, not Latin, form of the pope's name.

Conciliar Documents

Again, these documents are traditionally named using the first phrase of the document in Latin. These are standard names and should always be used.

First reference:

> [1]*Dei Verbum* (Dogmatic Constitution on Divine Revelation), Vatican Council II, November 18, 1965, no. 24.

Second and subsequent references:

> [2]*Dei Verbum*, no. 24.

Note that the titles of these documents are italicized. Documents from previous councils also follow the same format.

Writing about the Holocaust

The Holocaust, or Shoah, was the systematic murder of Jews throughout Europe during the Second World War, with the goal of eliminating the entire Jewish population of Europe. Writing about the Holocaust requires sensitivity to victims and survivors. Be aware that you are writing about an event that affected the whole world, not just people of the Jewish faith. Avoid any kind of implication that the victims of the Holocaust deserved their fate. This means avoiding stereotypes, especially the stereotypes spread by the perpetrators of genocide, such as the idea that Jews were destabilizing society or that they controlled many aspects of the financial system. Also avoid any false equivalence between the Holocaust and other events. The Holocaust was a unique event with unique consequences; it is not "just the same" as any other event, even any other incidence of genocide.

When writing about the concentration camps, use the generally accepted names and spellings: Auschwitz, Birkenau, Bergen-Belsen. Avoid writing casually or cavalierly about these places.

Terrorism

Avoid any language that implies an inherent connection between Islam and violence, especially terrorism. If terrorists describe themselves as Muslim or appeal to the tenets of Islam, offer the perspectives of people who disagree with their violent interpretations. To equip yourself to discuss Islam with accuracy, become familiar with the tenets of the faith, especially the religious concept of jihad. In Islam, jihad is the struggle to live as a believer and to create communities where social justice reigns. Understanding this concept will allow you to evaluate the statements of both criminals and those who offer arguments against them and to offer insightful analysis in your papers. Seek the help of your professor or teaching assistant to be sure you understand what's at stake and the major issues involved.

3

WRITING ABOUT RELIGIONS
Beyond the Abrahamic Traditions

This chapter continues the discussion begun in chapter 2 on writing about religions but shifts focus away from the Abrahamic religions toward other religions commonly studied by college students in the United States.

DEITIES

There are more than 1,500 religious traditions around the world, each with its own beliefs, ethics, and gods. Although the Abrahamic traditions are distinguished by their connection to Abraham and the belief that there is only one true God, many religious traditions have many gods, no god, or people who are revered as sages. Be sure you understand the concept of a god or gods in the faith you are writing about. Use reliable sources, such as sacred texts, commentaries, encyclopedias, and academic books and articles, to support your understanding.

Capitalize the names of any gods or revered persons as you would any proper noun. Use lowercase for the word *god* when writing about the gods of polytheistic faiths, but capitalize God for monotheistic faiths. Note, for example, that God is capitalized in Sikhism, which is monotheistic.

Spelling is something of an issue when writing about gods and goddesses whose names are transliterated from languages like Sanskrit, Pali, and Chinese: often there is no standard English spelling.

(The same challenge arises with types of terms such as *nirvana, samsara*, or *moksha*). Use the spellings you find in your research and be consistent throughout the paper, except where necessary in direct quotations. If the spelling differs among your sources (which often happens and should not be a source of great anxiety), use the more common spelling, or choose one spelling and use it consistently.

There are too many religious traditions to list all of their gods, goddesses, and beliefs. What follows are some faiths that are commonly the subjects of undergraduate papers. Consult your reference librarian for standard reference works on other faiths.

Hindu Divinities

Hinduism has many gods, goddesses, and godlike figures. The major gods are Brahma, Shiva, and Vishnu, who form the Trimurti. Other gods are usually avatars, or representations drawn from one of the figures of the Trimurti. Capitalize the names of the gods and Trimurti, but do not capitalize *avatar*. Be sure to check your source material for the names of the gods as many of them are similar. Some sources will place *lord* before the god's name. Do this in direct quotations, but it is not necessary otherwise. For example: Krishna, Rama, Devi, Kali, Ganesha.

Chinese Divinities

Chinese traditional religion, common throughout Asia, involves a complex system of gods, goddesses, ghosts, ancestors, and other beings. Be sure you understand the relationships among these beings before writing about them. Use the names as they appear in your research materials.

God in Sikhism

Sikhism is a monotheistic faith that draws its beliefs from elements of Hinduism and Islam. Sikhs call God by many different names, including Om-kara (the divine one), Satguru (true teacher), and Waheguru (wonderful teacher). Choose the term that appears most often in your research materials and use it consistently. Always capitalize each of these terms in relation to God. Each of these terms may also be used as common nouns, so do not capitalize them when they are not referring to God. The word *guru* is a common noun and is not capitalized when used in relation to human beings, except in rare cases when it is used as a title.

Shinto Divinities

In Shinto, the major religious tradition of Japan, the gods or divine spirits are called kami. Do not capitalize *kami*, but do capitalize the names of any specific kami, such as Amaterasu, the divine spirit of the sun, who is revered as the guardian of the Japanese people.

PEOPLE

Revered Persons

In addition to deities, and sometimes in place of deities, many faiths revere people who are good examples of the faith, people worthy of great respect, or people who have been important to the development of the faith. Always write about these people with respect, using their names and any titles normally attached to them by their religious tradition.

The Buddha

In Buddhism, Siddhartha Gautama is revered as the Buddha, a Sanskrit word meaning "awakened one" or "enlightened one." The name Siddhartha alone is sometimes used, and the full name can be spelled in different ways. The Buddha, the primary figure of Buddhism, is also sometimes known as Gautama Buddha or simply Buddha. Always capitalize Buddha in relation to this person, and be consistent in your choice of terms for him. Use the lowercase when discussing concepts such as buddha nature or buddha sense that do not refer directly to the Buddha. Instead, these terms refer to a disposition toward goodness or enlightenment.

Revered Figures of Confucianism

The philosophy known in the West as Confucianism presents some semantic challenges in referring to the most important figures in that tradition. (Note: Confucianism is more properly considered a philosophy than a religion. It is discussed in this guide because students in religion courses sometimes study it.) The name Confucius is an English corruption of the Chinese name Kong Fuzi, which means Master Kong. Likewise, the name of another important figure, Meng Zi, has been corrupted as Mencius. The most correct way to refer to these men in English would be as Master Kong (or Kung) and Master Meng. In China and other Chinese-influenced areas, the names most often used for them are Kongzi and Mengzi. However, it is conventional to refer to them in English as Confucius and Mencius. Choose one method and use it throughout your paper.

Laozi (Daoism)

Daoism respects Laozi as the author of the Daodejing, the most important writing in Daoism and a popular and important work to many nonreligious Chinese. You may also see his name written as Lao-tse or Lao-tzu. These constructions all refer to the same person. The difference in English spelling is because of a shift in the method of transliterating Chinese from the older Wade-Giles method to pinyin, a system for romanizing Chinese that was developed in the twentieth century. Choose one spelling and use it throughout your paper.

Guru Nanak (Sikhism)

The founder of Sikhism is Guru Nanak. Capitalize guru (teacher) in this case, but do not capitalize it when it is used as a common noun.

Rely on your sources and use your best judgment when writing about the revered religious figures. In general, capitalize both their names and their titles.

Leaders and Believers

Leaders of Groups or Sects

As in the Abrahamic traditions, most of the world's religions have divisions, groups, or sects. Many have leaders who can be thought of only as the leader of that group or sect, not of all of Buddhism, for example, or of all of Hinduism. Be careful to link the leader with the correct group. Groups can also have informal leaders, and the titles of those leaders are not capitalized. Some examples of titles include: lama, guru, master, seer.

Hindus

People who follow Hinduism are called Hindus. Some leaders are called gurus (teachers), but there is no overall universal Hindu leader.

▶▶ Hinduism is associated with the nation of India, but India is very religiously diverse. *Hindu* and *Indian* are not synonyms; not all Indians are Hindus. Also avoid labeling anyone as Hindu unless you are certain of his or her religious background. Personal names such as Krishna or Parvati (both names of Hindu gods that are common names for people) are not indicators of religious faith, just as the names David and Ruth do not indicate that a person is Jewish. ◄

Buddhists

People who follow the Buddha are known as Buddhists. Buddhism has many different sects with many different practices, but it is not usually necessary to distinguish among them unless it is relevant to the topic of your paper. Because Buddhism has the nature of a personal quest, it does not have an overall leader and very few leaders of any kind. Zen (Chan) Buddhism has teachers who are often called masters or priests. Capitalize *master* when it is used in conjunction with a specific name, such as Master Hiro, but not in other contexts.

The Dalai Lama is the leader of one branch of Buddhism, not the leader of all of Buddhism. A lama is a teacher, similar to a guru, and other than the Dalai Lama, the word *lama* should not be capitalized. The Dalai Lama is revered only by a small portion of Buddhists, so avoid implying that he speaks for all of Buddhism.

Some Buddhists live together in religious communities. They are properly known as monks and nuns. These terms are treated just as they are when referring to Christian monks and nuns: neither term is capitalized or used as a title. Unlike in Christianity, however, Buddhist monks and nuns are not known as "brothers" or "sisters."

Sikhs

The followers of Sikhism are known as Sikhs, a term that means "disciple." There are several Sikh groups, but these groups are not rigid or exclusive since a primary teaching of Sikhism is unity.

▶ Refer to your research and use common sense in determining how to refer to members of other religious groups around the world. ◀

TEXTS

In some religious traditions, such as Sikhism, texts are very important. In others, like Buddhism, religious texts are much less important, and often not important at all to ordinary believers. Be careful about how much significance you place on religious texts in your paper and be sure that you are using them properly.

▶ Never refer to the scriptures of religions other than Judaism or Christianity as "bibles." Only Christians and Jews have Bibles, and the role of scripture in Christianity and Judaism is different from the role of the scriptures of many other religious traditions. ◀

Hindu Texts

Hinduism has some of the world's oldest religious texts, significant both religiously and historically. The primary texts are the Vedas and the Upanishads, which include stories in prose, poem, and dialogue form. Hinduism's texts include two major epics, the Mahabharata and the Ramayana. A very famous section of the Mahabharata is the Bhagavad Gita. Other writings are less common but also significant. These include the Puranas, the Tantras, and the Laws of Manu. Notice that these titles are not italicized.

Be sure to identify clearly which Hindu texts you are referencing. There are several Vedas, including the Rig Veda, the Atharva Veda, and the Sama Veda. There are also many Upanishads. When quoting from any of the texts of the Hindu tradition, provide the title of the larger writing, the publication information, and the chapter, stanza, or line numbers of your quotation. The first reference to a text requires a footnote with all of the information, like this:

[6]All quotations from the Rig Veda are taken from Wendy Doniger, ed. and trans., *The Rig Veda* (London: Penguin Classics, 2005).

See chapter 4 for more on footnotes.

For subsequent references, provide a parenthetical citation that includes the chapter, stanza, or line numbers that will be most useful in locating your quotation. These numbers will often be in the margins of the text or will be marked throughout the text in some other way. Page numbers are not necessary. For example: "He who made fast the tottering earth, who made still the quaking mountains, who measured out and extended the expanse of the air, who propped up the sky—he, my people, is Indra." (Rig Veda 2.12)

Some scriptures, especially those that are more obscure, are collected in anthologies of world scriptures. These anthologies have selections from many different scriptures together in one book. If you use a selection from an anthology, use full information, including page numbers, in the footnotes. Use a footnote for every selection from an anthology, including page numbers.

Buddhist Texts

As with the Hindu tradition, the Buddhist tradition has many sacred texts. These texts include a wide variety of writings, none of which are accepted by all Buddhists. In writing about scripture in the Buddhist tradition, it is important to know which group or division within Buddhism you are discussing, because different texts are important to different groups. It would be incorrect to quote from the Pali canon, used by some Theravada Buddhists, in a paper about Zen, a form of Mahayana Buddhism. The two groups are very different.

The Pali canon, a collection of texts, is associated with Theravada Buddhism. This collection is referred to as the Tripitaka, a term meaning "three baskets," which reflects the fact that the text was originally written on leaves that were stored in baskets. Please note that today *Tripitaka* is used to refer to various collections, so be careful how you use the term. The Chinese canon is important throughout East Asia, and the Kangyur is a standard of Tibetan Buddhism. Many different writings are used in Zen Buddhism that are not used in other sects, especially the writings about koans and some writings on meditation.

To quote from any of the texts of Buddhism, follow the same forms for footnotes, chapter, line, and stanza numbers as outlined for Hinduism.

Confucian Texts

Confucianism is a philosophy that reveres several major texts, especially the Analects of Confucius, the Five Classics, and the Four Books. These are standard names given to different groups of writings. The Analects are consistently numbered by section, so cite them using the same guidelines outlined above for the Vedas. Use a full footnote for the first reference, then section numbers within the text for every reference after that.

For the other major works of Confucianism, including the Yijing and the remaining Classics and Books, follow the rules for nonreligious books as outlined in chapter 4, including publication information and page numbers. There are many different translations of these works, and the numbering and titles can differ from translation to translation.

Daoist Texts

The Daodejing is the primary writing of Daoism, although there are many others. Treat works other than the Daodejing as you would any other nonreligious book, using footnotes, complete publication information, and page numbers. The Daodejing itself is cited as noted above for the Rig Veda: use a footnote with full publication information for the first reference, and after that use the section numbers from the Daodejing. There are many, many different translations of the Daodejing, so the translation and publication date are especially important. Most professors have a preferred translation, so use the one assigned for class, or ask your professor or teaching assistant for help in finding a good translation.

▶▶ Many translations of the Daodejing are available for free on the Internet. Do not use these for academic work. The translation of the Daodejing is complex, both because of the original language and because of the ideas expressed, and a good academic translation is essential. Small differences in translation can make for different nuances of meaning in the work. Ask your professor to recommend a good translation. ◂

Sikh Texts

The major religious text of Sikhism is the Adi Granth, the "first book" of the Sikhs. The Adi Granth is sometimes written about as the Guru Granth Sahib, the "revered teacher, the Granth." Be aware of this term in your reading. Usually, any writer who refers to "the revered teacher" will be referring to the Adi Granth.

The Adi Granth has three major divisions, the most important of which is the Japji, the first division of hymns. Anything that is referred to as coming from the Japji will be from the Adi Granth.

There are several complete translations of the Adi Granth, as well as some books that are translations of selections of hymns from the Adi Granth. Because there are many different publications and selections, use footnotes with page numbers for every quotation from the Adi Granth.

▸ Many of the sacred texts of other world faiths will follow the same rules as nonreligious books. Be sure of what you are reading and use common sense along with the guidelines offered here to cite your materials properly. ◂

RELIGIOUS SERVICES AND RITES

World religions observe a wide variety of religious services. All of these are properly referred to as services, although not all of them are worship. Be careful about using the word *worship* unless you are certain that this is the intended purpose of a service or ritual. Also be careful about suggesting that people of a particular religious or spiritual tradition worship other people, statues, or other objects. For example, some Buddhists and Jains may worship at statues but they are not worshipping the statues. The statues are a venue for worship, not an object of worship. This is similar to the Christian practice of praying at statues of Mary, for example, or of using religious icons of the saints as an aid to prayer.

Hindus, Buddhists, Jains, and some Daoists hold services at temples. These temples can have individual names, which should be capitalized. Sikh houses of worship can be called temples in English, but are more properly called gurdwaras. Generally, it is best to use the name that the group in question uses. Buddhism and some other faiths may also have meditation centers, meditation temples, or Buddhist centers. Again, give the names used by the people or groups who have established the temples or centers.

Capitalize the names of holidays and generally celebrated festivals, but not most services. The differences between holidays and regular services can be difficult to determine if you are not familiar with a faith, so do careful research. Some faiths, such as Hinduism and some aspects of Chinese traditional religion, may refer to such occasions as "auspicious days" instead of holidays. Be aware that not all divisions of any one faith celebrate the same holidays or festivals and that there are real differences in religious understandings that determine whether a holiday or festival is celebrated. For example, some Buddhists celebrate the birth of the Buddha, while others do not.

> Hindu festivals and holidays include the following: Holi, Diwali, Durga Puja, Maha Shivrati, Rathyatra
>
> Buddhist festivals include the following: New Year, Mangha Puja, Hanamatsuri, Vesak

RELIGIOUS CONCEPTS

In some faiths, major religious concepts are capitalized to set them apart from similar but lesser concepts in the same faith. Capitalize them only when referring to the overall important major concept and to set them apart from similar concepts. The goal is to reflect the usage within the faith itself. For example, within Buddhism, the dharma is one's way of life, the ethics and obligations of living with others. The Dharma, however, is the universal moral law that binds all creatures together. The difference is significant.

Some concepts that can be distinguished this way include: enlightenment and Enlightenment, dharma and Dharma, karma and Karma, and truth and the Truth.

HEAVEN IN CHINESE TRADITIONS

Confucianism and Chinese traditional religion (sometimes called ancestor worship or folk religion) include a concept called Heaven (tian). This is not the same as the Christian concept of heaven. Heaven in Chinese traditions is somewhat difficult to define as it can refer to several different things. Most often it is referred to as an amorphous power that is associated with the ancestors, and sometimes with the gods and goddesses of the Chinese tradition. Some writings and religious understandings mark Heaven as the realm of Shang-ti, the Supreme Ruler. (Note that Shang-ti is not the same as the Abrahamic concept of God.) The most important concept associated with Heaven is the Mandate of Heaven (tianming), through which rulers are given divine permission to rule and continue to rule through the practice of the Chinese virtues, not by any rights of their own.

Always capitalize Heaven in relation to the Chinese concept.

HINDU CASTES

A major feature of Hinduism is the caste system. The caste system represents a hierarchy of karmic attainment, and Hindus believe that beings make spiritual progress by moving up this hierarchy. Each caste has a name, and you should use those names consistently. Capitalize the names of the castes, and use the spellings most common in your research, for example, Brahmin, Kshitriya, Vaishya, and Shudra.

There is another class of people traditionally known as the untouchables. This class falls below the four castes, and its members have the worst karma. Avoid using *untouchables* in your papers except in direct quotations, as some people consider it offensive. Avoid the terms *outcaste* and *slumdog*, both common terms for members of the lowest class, for the same reason. Use the actual title of the class, which is usually Dalit, Harijan, or Ashprush, depending on the language involved.

4

CITING SOURCES

Citation, the process of documenting the sources used in researching and writing, is one of the most important elements in a paper. It serves three purposes: to give credit to the people whose work you use, to give readers the information needed to locate your research materials, and to provide support for the positions you articulate in your paper.

WHEN TO CITE

Include a citation—a footnote, endnote, or in-text citation—whenever you use someone else's work. This includes direct quotations as well as indirect quotations or paraphrases. Also use a citation whenever you use another person's original idea, even if your description uses completely different wording. Facts that are not common knowledge and that you learn from research (such as statistics or demographic information) should also be footnoted.

Do not use footnotes for common knowledge or for material gathered from dictionaries, thesauruses, or other reference books.

▶Common knowledge refers to facts or concepts that many people know or that appear in many sources. For example, the date of the Declaration of Independence (1776) is common knowledge. The definitions of most words are also common knowledge and don't require footnoting within the paper. ◄

SYSTEMS FOR CITING SOURCES

There are different systems for documenting sources. This chapter describes and provides examples for the two systems preferred by the University of Chicago Press: the note-bibliography system and the author-date system. In your studies, especially outside of religion and theology, you may encounter other systems, including those of the Modern Language Association, the American Psychological Association, or the American Medical Association. The different systems for documenting sources and the styles that govern how particular elements in a citation are written require most of the same information about your sources.

▶ Always be sure to use the documentation system (e.g., the note-bibliography system or the author-date system) your professor advises. Clarify the allowable options before you begin. Using a different system from the one required by your professor can result in a lower grade. Most college libraries have a reference librarian who can help you, and many have computer programs that will help you properly format and organize your citations. College writing centers are also good places to look for help with citation. Trust these people to guide you correctly rather than consulting the Internet, which may not offer the kind of information you need or could cause you to insert errors into your papers. ◄

Though this chapter describes the two documentation systems preferred by *The Chicago Manual of Style*, it gives more attention to the note-bibliography system, which uses notes at the bottom of a page or at the end of a paper and a bibliography. This is because most publications in the area of religion and theology use this system, and many religion and theology professors prefer it. Because some publications and professors prefer the author-date system, which uses an in-text parenthetical citation and a works-cited page, basic information about this system is provided as well. Whichever system you use, use it consistently and properly throughout the paper.

Only the most commonly cited types of materials are covered in this chapter. For information about citing other materials, such as music and movies, see *The Chicago Manual of Style: The Essential Guide for Writers, Editors, and Publishers*, 16th ed. (Chicago: University of Chicago Press, 2010) or Kate L. Turabian et al., *A Manual for Writers of Research Papers, Theses, and Dissertations: Chicago Style for Students and Researchers,* 7th ed. (Chicago: University of Chicago Press, 2007).

The Note-Bibliography System of Documentation

This method of citation uses footnotes or endnotes and a bibliography at the end of the paper. It is the method most often used in the study of religion and in some other disciplines in the social sciences.

Keep in mind that there is a difference between a documentation system, such as the note-bibliography system, and a style. Style here refers to the format used for citations. This encompasses the use of mechanics such as punctuation, capitalization, abbreviations, and parentheses. When this guide provides a sample cite in the note-bibliography system, it notes two style options. The first is the style called for by *The Chicago Manual of Style* and the second is a simplified style adapted from the Chicago style. Use one or the other consistently, after learning if your professor has a preference.

Footnote and Endnote Formatting

Footnotes appear at the bottom of the page; endnotes are grouped together at the end of the paper. Most word processing programs can accommodate either format. Decide whether you will use footnotes or endnotes and then stick with that format throughout the paper. Be consistent and don't mix the two styles.

Number your footnotes or endnotes consecutively from the beginning of your document using Arabic numerals (1, 2, 3 . . .), not Roman numerals or symbols. Use the same typeface as the rest of your paper, in a readable type size.

Each footnote should receive a separate number. Numbers should not be repeated, even if they refer to the same source. See the section below on citing the same source several times.

Placement of Footnotes or Endnotes in the Text

Footnotes or endnotes are marked with a superscript numeral at the end of the sentence, after the final punctuation (such as a period).

This is an example of the placement of a footnote reference number.[1]

Notes can also be placed in the middle of a complex sentence, after the punctuation, if the material referred to falls within the first clause of the sentence:

> Some footnotes are placed in the middle of a sentence,[1] if the material warrants it.

Bibliographies

A bibliography is a list of all the sources consulted for the paper. It is different from a "works cited" page in the author-date system in that it includes all materials consulted for the paper, not just those that are specifically cited. Anything that you read to prepare for the paper—all of the articles, books, and other materials used in your research—need to be listed in the bibliography, with the exception of general dictionaries, general encyclopedias, and thesauruses. Specialized dictionaries and encyclopedias, such as the Anchor Bible Dictionary and the Catholic Encyclopedia, do need to be cited. Whenever you are unsure about the need to cite a source, it is best to do so.

There are a few small differences between the styles for notes and bibliography entries. The primary difference is that footnotes and endnotes refer to the author by first name and then surname, while bibliographies list surnames first. A bibliography is alphabetized by surname.

List all the sources for your bibliography separately from the body of the paper and from the endnotes. Begin the bibliography on a new sheet of paper; don't begin the bibliography at the bottom of the last page of your essay.

Citing Printed Sources

Printed sources and digitized versions of print sources such as e-books and scholarly journals that are published online are treated essentially the same. (See the section on Internet sources below for more information on e-books and journals found through online databases.) The examples of notes and bibliographic entries that follow show how to refer to the printed materials used most frequently by undergraduates.

Note

Chicago:

[1]Peter Feldmeier, *Encounters in Faith: Christianity in Inter-religious Dialogue* (Winona, MN: Anselm Academic, 2011), 157.

Simplified:

[1]Peter Feldmeier, *Encounters in Faith: Christianity in Inter-religious Dialogue.* Winona, MN: Anselm Academic, 2011, 157.

▶ Notice the different use of punctuation, abbreviations, and parentheses in the above examples. Follow the examples carefully for whichever style you are using. These are differences in style. ◄

Bibliography

Chicago:

Feldmeier, Peter. *Encounters in Faith: Christianity in Interreligious Dialogue.* Winona, MN: Anselm Academic, 2011.

Simplified:

Feldmeier, Peter, *Encounters in Faith: Christianity in Interreligious Dialogue.* Winona, MN: Anselm Academic, 2011.

Using names

When listing any author, editor, or translator's name, use the form of the name *exactly* as it appears on the cover of the book or the title page, even if the same author uses other forms of his or her name in other works. Be careful to note the use (or nonuse) of middle initials, academic titles such as PhD, and religious affiliations listed after a person's name: if the author includes this information, so should you.

Compound Surnames

Respecting people means using their names correctly, the way that people prefer their names to be used. Many people have two surnames that they use consistently as a double surname, with or without a hyphen linking them. This is especially common in Asian and Spanish surnames, although many people in the United States have begun using two surnames as well, whether hyphenated or not. Some authors use an Asian construction for their names, listing the surname first and their personal names following that. It is sometimes impossible to tell which names are a part of a compound surname and which names the person in question considers a middle name. Some examples:

Elisabeth Schussler Fiorenza

Kwok Pui Lan

Lisa Sowle Cahill

David Matzko McCarthy

Mari Rapela Heidt

Ada Maria Isasi-Diaz

Bartolomé de las Casas

Jung Young Lee

The best course of action for deciding where to divide names for an alphabetical bibliography listing or a bibliography entry is to check the cataloging information at an academic library. The listing for that author will generally be correctly divided and alphabetized. The above examples are divided in this way:

Schussler Fiorenza, Elisabeth

Kwok, Pui lan

Cahill, Lisa Sowle

McCarthy, David Matzko

Rapela Heidt, Mari

Isasi-Diaz, Ada Maria

Las Casas, Bartolomé de

Lee, Jung Young

Religious Offices or Affiliations

In general, use the religious office or affiliation in footnotes, endnotes, or bibliography entries if it appears on the cover or title page of any written work. Do not insert titles for authors or editors, even if you know them. For example, give the name of the author as "Cardinal Joseph Bernardin" if it appears this way on the cover of the work you have consulted, but do not insert "Cardinal" before the author "Joseph Bernardin" if it does not appear on the cover or title page *even if you know that the author was in fact a cardinal when he wrote this work.* Likewise, one would use "His Holiness the Dalai Lama" as the author if it appears this way on the cover or title page of a written work, even if you are not a Buddhist or don't believe that the Dalai Lama is holy.

Many authors or editors who belong to religious communities list abbreviations for those communities after their names. Include these as a part of the author's or editor's name in any entry, like this: Benedict Guevin, OSB, Philip S. Keane, S.S., and Mark Massa, S.J. Use periods or other punctuation exactly as used by the person in question. If you find that some of your sources use periods and some do not, choose one style and use it consistently. Follow the directions of your professor or teaching assistant.

Book with One Author

Note

Chicago:

²³Anthony Burke Smith, *The Look of Catholics: Portrayals in Popular Culture from the Great Depression to the Cold War* (Lawrence, KS: University of Kansas Press, 2010), 43.

Simplified:

²³Anthony Burke Smith, *The Look of Catholics: Portrayals in Popular Culture from the Great Depression to the Cold War.* Lawrence, KS: University of Kansas Press, 2010, 43.

Bibliography

Chicago:

Smith, Anthony Burke. *The Look of Catholics: Portrayals in Popular Culture from the Great Depression to the Cold War.* Lawrence, KS: University of Kansas Press, 2010.

Smith, Anthony Burke, *The Look of Catholics: Portrayals in Popular Culture from the Great Depression to the Cold War.* Lawrence, KS: University of Kansas Press, 2010.

Book with Two or Three Authors

For a book with more than one author, list the authors in the order they appear on the book cover or title page. Notice that the author names are not always alphabetized.

Note

Chicago:

[21]Catherine M. Barsotti and Robert K. Johnston, *Finding God in the Movies: 33 Films of Reel Faith* (Grand Rapids, MI: Baker Books, 2004), 174.

Simplified:

[21]Catherine M. Barsotti and Robert K. Johnston, *Finding God in the Movies: 33 Films of Reel Faith.* Grand Rapids, MI: Baker Books, 2004, 174.

Bibliography

Chicago:

Barsotti, Catherine M., and Robert K. Johnston. *Finding God in the Movies: 33 Films of Reel Faith.* Grand Rapids, MI: Baker Books, 2004.

Simplified:

Barsotti, Catherine M., and Robert K. Johnston, *Finding God in the Movies: 33 Films of Reel Faith.* Grand Rapids, MI: Baker Books, 2004.

Book with More than Three Authors

Books with more than three authors will list only the first named author and then note that he or she is not the sole author by including the term *and others* or its Latin abbreviation, *et al.*

Note

Chicago:

> [19]Nancy C. Ring et al., *Introduction to the Study of Religion.* Maryknoll, NY: Orbis Books, 1998, 32.

Simplified:

> [19]Nancy C. Ring and others, *Introduction to the Study of Religion.* Maryknoll, NY: Orbis Books, 1998, 32.

Bibliography

Chicago:

Ring, Nancy C., et al. *Introduction to the Study of Religion.* Maryknoll, NY: Orbis Books, 1998.

Simplified:

Ring, Nancy C., and others, *Introduction to the Study of Religion.* Maryknoll, NY: Orbis Books, 1998.

Book with an Editor instead of an Author

If no single author is listed, treat edited books as though the editor is the author; include the designation "ed." to indicate that the person listed is an editor, not an author.

Book with a Single Editor

Note

Chicago:

> [13]Willis Barnstone, ed., *The Other Bible: Ancient Alternative Scriptures* (San Francisco: Harper San Francisco, 1984), 253.

Simplified:

[13]Willis Barnstone, ed., *The Other Bible: Ancient Alternative Scriptures.* San Francisco: Harper San Francisco, 1984, 253.

Bibliography

Chicago:

Barnstone, Willis, ed. *The Other Bible: Ancient Alternative Scriptures.* San Francisco: Harper San Francisco, 1984.

Simplified:

Barnstone, Willis, ed., *The Other Bible, Ancient Alternative Scriptures.* San Francisco: Harper San Francisco, 1984.

Book with Multiple Editors

As with a book with multiple authors, list the editors as they are listed on the book cover or title page, noting after the names that they are editors, not authors. Note that they may not be in alphabetical order.

Note

Chicago:

[24]David Matzko McCarthy and M. Therese Lysaught, eds., *Gathered for the Journey: Moral Theology in Catholic Perspective* (Grand Rapids, MI: Eerdmans, 2007), 179.

Simplified:

[24]David Matzko McCarthy and M. Therese Lysaught, eds., *Gathered for the Journey: Moral Theology in Catholic Perspective.* Grand Rapids, MI: Eerdmans, 2007, 179.

Bibliography

Chicago:

McCarthy, David Matzko, and M. Therese Lysaught, eds. *Gathered for the Journey: Moral Theology in Catholic Perspective.* Grand Rapids, MI: Eerdmans, 2007.

Simplified:

McCarthy, David Matzko, and M. Therese Lysaught, eds., *Gathered for the Journey: Moral Theology in Catholic Perspective.* Grand Rapids, MI: Eerdmans, 2007.

Book with an Author and an Editor

For books with an author and an editor, list the author's name first, then the editor.

Note

Chicago:

[32]Cardinal Joseph Bernardin, *The Seamless Garment: Writings on the Consistent Ethic of Life,* ed. Thomas A. Nairn (Maryknoll, NY: Orbis Books, 2008), 238.

Simplified:

[32]Cardinal Joseph Bernardin, *The Seamless Garment: Writings on the Consistent Ethic of Life,* ed. by Thomas A. Nairn. Maryknoll, NY: Orbis Books, 2008, 238.

Bibliography

Chicago:

Bernardin, Cardinal Joseph. *The Seamless Garment: Writings on the Consistent Ethic of Life.* Edited by Thomas A. Nairn. Maryknoll, NY: Orbis Books, 2008.

Simplified:

Bernardin, Cardinal Joseph, *The Seamless Garment: Writings on the Consistent Ethic of Life.* Edited by Thomas A. Nairn. Maryknoll, NY: Orbis Books, 2008.

Book with a Translator

The citation for a translated book needs to list both the author and the translator. The author is listed first in the citation, with the translator clearly identified and separate from the author. In the bibliography, alphabetize by the author's name, not the translator's. If a book has both and editor and a translator, list the editor before the translator.

Note

Chicago:

[1]Leonardo Boff, *Cry of the Earth, Cry of the Poor,* trans. Phillip Berryman (Maryknoll, NY: Orbis Books, 1997), 26.

Simplified:

[1]Leonardo Boff, *Cry of the Earth, Cry of the Poor,* trans. by Phillip Berryman. Maryknoll, NY: Orbis Books, 1997, 26.

Bibliography

Chicago:

Boff, Leonardo. *Cry of the Earth, Cry of the Poor.* Translated by Phillip Berryman. Maryknoll, NY: Orbis Books, 1997.

Simplified:

Boff, Leonardo, *Cry of the Earth, Cry of the Poor.* Translated by Phillip Berryman. Maryknoll, NY: Orbis Books, 1997.

Book with a Question as a Main Title

Some books use a question as the main title of the work. The question mark at the end of the main title is not followed by a colon or other punctuation when a subtitle follows.

Note

Chicago:

[16]Mark J. Allman, *Who Would Jesus Kill? War, Peace, and the Christian Tradition* (Winona, MN: Anselm Academic, 2008), 122.

Simplified:

[16]Mark J. Allman, *Who Would Jesus Kill? War, Peace, and the Christian Tradition.* Winona, MN: Anselm Academic, 2008, 122.

Bibliography

Chicago:

Allman, Mark J. *Who Would Jesus Kill? War, Peace, and the Christian Tradition.* Winona, MN: Anselm Academic, 2008.

Simplified:

Allman, Mark J., *Who Would Jesus Kill? War, Peace, and the Christian Tradition.* Winona, MN: Anselm Academic, 2008.

Chapters in Books

Refer to chapters in books in a separate footnote or bibliography entry when the chapter is titled and an author is named. This will usually occur only in a collection of essays. As a general rule, in a book by a single author you do not need to refer to, for example, chapter 3, in a separate note, even if the chapters have separate titles. In an edited volume, the chapters or other divisions within the book will usually have been written by different authors and will have separate titles and will need separate notes and bibliography entries.

Note

Chicago:

[16]Ann Marie Hsiung, "Gender and Same-Sex Relations in Confucianism and Taoism," in *Heterosexism in Contemporary World Religion*, ed. Marvin M. Ellison and Judith Plaskow (Cleveland, OH: The Pilgrim Press, 2007), 104.

Simplified:

[16]Ann Marie Hsiung, "Gender and Same-Sex Relations in Confucianism and Taoism," in *Heterosexism in Contemporary World Religion*, ed. Marvin M. Ellison and Judith Plaskow. Cleveland, OH: The Pilgrim Press, 2007, 104.

Bibliography

Chicago:

Hsiung, Ann Marie. "Gender and Same-Sex Relations in Confucianism and Taoism." In *Heterosexism in Contemporary*

World Religion, edited by Marvin M. Ellison and Judith Plaskow, 104–17. Cleveland, OH: The Pilgrim Press, 2007.

Simplified:

Hsiung, Ann Marie, "Gender and Same-Sex Relations in Confucianism and Taoism," in *Heterosexism in Contemporary World Religion*, ed. Marvin M. Ellison and Judith Plaskow, Cleveland, OH: The Pilgrim Press, 2007, 104–117.

Books in Foreign Languages

Treat books in languages other than English exactly as you would books written in English. It is not necessary to translate titles or other parts of the entry. If you have also used a translated version of the book along with the one in the original language, you will need to enter both in the bibliography.

▶▶ Be especially careful about spelling and diacritical marks in foreign languages. Diacritical marks are accent marks that appear above or below letters in some languages that indicate the sound of the letter. Check them twice, as improperly placed marks can change the meanings of words. For example, many men around the world are named Jesús, a popular name in Spanish. It can also be used in some places as a surname. Jesús is very different from Jesus! ◄

E-Books

Many books are available electronically in different formats for different e-readers and computer platforms. These books should still have publication data and should be treated much the same as a printed book. The only difference comes in how the publication information is presented.

Bibliography

Chicago:

Smith, Huston. *The Soul of Christianity: Restoring the Great Tradition*. New York: HarperCollins, 2009. Kindle edition.

Simplified:

Smith, Huston, *The Soul of Christianity: Restoring the Great Tradition*. New York: HarperCollins e-book, 2009.

Notice that this is the same information and format as for a printed book, with the inclusion of "Kindle edition" or equivalent (for Chicago style) or "e-book" (for simplified style) in the publication information. This alerts readers that some of the page numbers may be different from those in the paper work or that page numbers will be missing entirely.

The issue of page numbers in e-books is significant, as one of the goals of citation is to help others find your information quickly and easily. If page numbers are not available in your e-book edition, in a footnote or endnote where you would ordinarily list the page number, instead list the chapter or section where your information can be found. This is less precise than a page number but is of some use to others.

Note

Chicago:

¹⁴Huston Smith, *The Soul of Christianity: Restoring the Great Tradition* (New York: HarperCollins, 2009), Kindle ed., chap. 1.

Simplified:

¹⁴Huston Smith, *The Soul of Christianity: Restoring the Great Tradition*. New York: HarperCollins e-book, 2009, chapter 1, section titled "The Spirit of the Lord is upon me."

For e-books without publication information (which is hard to imagine), replace the publication information with the designation "e-book." It is to your advantage to try looking up the book on the website where it was purchased or in other places on the Internet to find publication information. Some will question the legitimacy of e-books without any kind of publication information. Evaluate the trustworthiness of e-books as sources in the same way that you weigh the value of any other source. If you do not have enough information about the author or the publisher, reconsider whether this is a good source for your paper, and also consider whether the same information can be found in more reliable sources or in printed editions of the same work.

Periodicals and Journals

Academic journals and other related periodicals are important within the study of religion and should be a large part of your research. Citing journals and periodicals is a bit different from citing books, primarily because periodical citations require volume and issue numbers along with dates. For example, suppose you find an article in the journal *Theological Studies*. This journal is published several times a year and has been publishing since 1940. It is insufficient to simply provide the title. You must also give the year and the issue number for that year so that the proper issue of the journal that contains your article can be found.

Computerized databases are now the easiest and most reliable way to locate materials. These databases and search engines—like JSTOR, Ebsco, and Proquest—are *not* a part of the citation for the articles and journals but are only a way of locating materials. They are the functional equivalent of the old card catalogs that once took up a great deal of room in every library and listed information on small cards. This means that your citations for articles should not include website information like "www.proquest.com" or "www.ebscohost.com." These references are to the search engine, not the article, and you want to include information specific to the article in your footnotes. No matter how you found the article in a journal, concentrate on including information that is specific to the article and will help a reader locate that article, regardless of the database the reader is using. This means that for every article you use, you will need the same basic information: the author's name, the title of the article, the title of the journal in which it was published, and the date of publication. You should also be sure to find the volume and issue numbers of the journal. Much of this information will be readily available in the listing provided by the search engine.

Articles in Academic Journals

Provide as much information as possible about the publication, including the volume number, the issue number (if there is one), and page numbers within the citation to ensure that it's clear where the article came from so that a reader can locate the article quickly and efficiently.

Note

Chicago:

[29]Joseph Kallarangatt, "St. Thomas Christians of India: Ecclesiological Heritages and Perspectives before the 17th Century," *Christian Orient* 14, no. 1 (1989): 23–40.

Simplified:

[29]Joseph Kallarangatt, "St. Thomas Christians of India: Ecclesiological Heritages and Perspectives before the 17th Century." *Christian Orient* vol. 14, no. 1 (1989), 23–40.

Bibliography

Chicago:

Kallarangatt, Joseph. "St. Thomas Christians of India: Ecclesiological Heritages and Perspectives before the 17th Century." *Christian Orient* 14, no. 1 (1989): 23–40.

Simplified:

Kallarangatt, Joseph, "St. Thomas Christians of India: Ecclesiological Heritages and Perspectives before the 17th Century." *Christian Orient* vol. 14, no. 1 (1989), 23–40.

In these examples, the author is listed first, then the title of the article. The title of the journal is italicized, followed by the volume number (14), a comma, the issue number (1), and then the date in parentheses. All of this information is necessary to locate the actual article being cited. The page numbers complete the entry. Unlike complete books, page numbers are kept for the bibliography entries for articles. It may be helpful to refer to the information provided by the search engine you used in locating the article.

Notice that there is no Web address following this entry, even though it was located through a database. Articles are best located by the information presented here: the author, the title of the article, and the journal in which it appears. Long strings of letters and numbers are confusing and unnecessary. The title of the database is also unnecessary, because citing the database is a bit like citing the specific card catalog where you found the entry for the article. The date you accessed the material is also unnecessary, as article and journal titles do not change from day to day.

Magazine and Newspaper Articles

Many articles from nonacademic sources can contribute to the success of a paper. For articles from magazines and newspapers, include all of the information that will help a reader quickly locate the material. Usually this will include the name of the author, the title of the article, the name of the publication in which it appears, the page numbers and the date of publication. As noted above, do not include the information about the search engine that you used to locate the article.

Note

Chicago:

⁴Gregory Pence, "Let's Think outside the Box of Bad Cliches," *Newsweek*, August 6, 2007, 17.

Simplified:

Identical to the above.

Bibliography

Chicago:

Pence, Gregory. "Let's Think outside the Box of Bad Cliches." *Newsweek*, August 6, 2007, 17.

Simplified:

Pence, Gregory, "Let's Think outside the Box of Bad Cliches," *Newsweek*, August 6, 2007, 17.

In simplified style, newspaper and magazine articles are treated the same way in footnotes and bibliography entries, except that the author's surname is listed first in the bibliography.

Citing Internet Sources

The Internet hosts a great deal of information, some of it legitimate and some of it not. Some publications on the Internet may provide useful information for the development of ideas and papers. All information from the Internet must be properly cited and credit given when you use it within your papers.

If articles are unsigned and from websites that end in .com, .biz, .info, or any other domain that is open to commercial purposes, you may want to reconsider using them in your paper. Be sure to review the information from chapter 1 on using the Internet in research.

Chicago style does not require access dates—the dates on which writers consulted online sources—in citations. Many professors, however, require students to note access dates in their papers. Access dates are of limited value in published works, but they may be helpful to professors and peers who read your papers. It is best to record access dates while doing research and to verify your professor's requirements.

Signed Article on a Website

An article with a named author on a website is treated in much the same way as the same type of article in a printed publication.

Note

Chicago:

[1]Dahlia Lithwick, "Bless Their Hearts," *Slate*, October 31, 2008, www.slate.com.

Simplified:

[1]Dahlia Lithwick, "Bless Their Hearts," *Slate*, October 31, 2008. Online at www.slate.com.

In this example, the author is listed first, the website itself is treated as a publication, and the website information takes the place of any publication information. Include as much material in the citation as necessary to help the reader find the article.

Unsigned Article on a Website

For an unsigned article on a website, treat the owner or producer of the website as the author.

Note

Chicago:

> [1]Bureau of Labor Statistics, "Wages in the Non-Profit Sector," October 2008, www.bls.gov.

Simplified:

> [1]Bureau of Labor Statistics, "Wages in the Non-Profit Sector," October 2008 report. Online at www.bls.gov.

▶ If you cannot determine a website's owner or sponsor, be cautious about using it as a reference for your paper. ◀

Online Articles from Magazines and Newspapers

Treat these the same way you would a printed copy of the newspaper or magazine. Include all of the publication information, but also include website information.

Note

Chicago:

> [7]Gregory Pence, "Let's Think outside the Box of Bad Cliches," *Newsweek*, August 6, 2007, 17, www.msnbc.msn.com/id/19999629/site/newsweek.com.

Simplified:

> [7]Gregory Pence, "Let's Think outside the Box of Bad Cliches," *Newsweek*, August 6, 2007, 17. Online at www. msnbc. msn.com.

Online Encyclopedias, Dictionaries, and Other Reference Materials

Recall that most general information dictionaries and thesauruses do not need to be cited, as the definitions of words and general facts are considered common knowledge. The same is true of online dictionaries and most other reference material. The exceptions are specialized dictionaries within a discipline. General information encyclopedias, such as the *Encyclopedia Brittanica*, in print or online, should also not be used in a serious collegiate paper. They are sometimes good for beginning background information, but little else. If you must cite them in a paper, treat them as signed or unsigned articles and note the websites carefully. Again, specialized encyclopedias specifically related to religion are the exception.

Citing the Same Source More than Once

Each time a source is used within the paper, it must be separately cited, with its own note number and reference. This is true even if you are referring to the same source several times.

To cite the same source more than once, include all of the information necessary, including the publication information, in the first footnote. If the notes that follow immediately are from the same source, write *Ibid.* (Latin for "in the same place"). If you are referring to the same book and same page as the previous note, ibid. alone is sufficient. If you are citing the same book but a different page, write *Ibid.* followed by the new page number. Do not use ibid. unless the work you cite is cited in the immediately preceding footnote. Here is an example of a set of three notes that refer to the same source:

Chicago:

¹Mari Rapela Heidt, *Moral Traditions: An Introduction to World Religious Ethics* (Winona, MN: Anselm Academic, 2010), 40.

²Ibid.

³Ibid., 42.

Simplified:

¹Mari Rapela Heidt, *Moral Traditions: An Introduction to World Religious Ethics*. Winona, MN: Anselm Academic, 2010, 40.

²Rapela Heidt, 40.

³Rapela Heidt, 42.

▶ Some professors today view the use of ibid. as archaic, as does the author of this text, as illustrated in the Simplified example above.

If that is the case with your professor, then in place of ibid. write the author's surname, and the page number. ◄

Some older works use the designation *op. cit.* to indicate that a full citation has already been given previously, with other citations between the previous full citation and the new one. Many now view the use of *op. cit.* as archaic, and it is falling out of use. Instead of using *op. cit.*, create a note that includes the author's surname, a short version of the source's title, and the page number. Here is an example of two citations from the same source, when a citation from another source intervenes.

Chicago:

> [1]Peter Feldmeier, *Encounters in Faith: Christianity in Interreligious Dialogue* (Winona, MN: Anselm Academic, 2011), 157.
>
> [2]Mari Rapela Heidt, *Moral Traditions: An Introduction to World Religious Ethics* (Winona, MN: Anselm Academic, 2010), 40.
>
> [3]Feldmeier, *Encounters*, 189.

Simplified:

> [1]Peter Feldmeier, *Encounters in Faith: Christianity in Interreligious Dialogue.* Winona, MN: Anselm Academic, 2011, 157.
>
> [2]Mari Rapela Heidt, *Moral Traditions: An Introduction to World Religious Ethics.* Winona, MN: Anselm Academic, 2010, 40.
>
> [3]Feldmeier, *Encounters,* 189.

► Even if all of your footnotes come from the same source, you must cite them separately. If the majority of your notes refer to the same source, consider whether you should consult additional sources. ◄

Informative or Explanatory Notes

In a complex paper involving a lot of research, there may be material tangential to the topic of the paper that will help the reader understand a point or offer secondary, but valuable, information. This material can be included in an explanatory footnote or endnote. Use this type of note when the extra information would enhance the reader's understanding. In terms of numbering and placement, treat them as you would any other note. See the sample endnotes for examples of explanatory notes.

Sample Endnotes

The following shows the endnotes for a typical research paper. Footnotes for the same paper would look exactly the same but would appear at the bottom of the pages on which the footnoted material appears, instead of being grouped together at the end of the paper. Notice the different features: each citation gets its own endnote even when information is taken from the same source, short titles are used on second reference to a work, the notes are consecutively numbered in standard numerals, and all of the notes follow the same format. Note that endnotes 1, 3, 5, 7, 12, 17, 19, and 20 are examples of simple first references; endnotes 2, 18, and 21 are examples of explanatory notes; and the rest are examples of second or subsequent references.

Chicago:

[1]Bailey W. Diffie and George D. Winius, *Foundations of the Portuguese Empire 1415–1580*, Europe and the World in the Age of Expansion 1 (Minneapolis: University of Minnesota Press, 1977), 181.

[2]For more on the Jesuits in India, see Teutonio R. de Souza and Charles J. Borges, eds., *Jesuits in India: In Historical Perspective* (Goa: Xavier Center of Historical Research, 1992).

[3]Paulo da Trindade, *Conquista Espiritual do Oriente*, ed. Felix Lopes (Lisbon: Centro de Estudos Historicos Ultramarinos, 1962), 82.

[4]Diffie and Winius, *Foundations*, 9.

[5]Sanjay Subrahmanyam, *The Portuguese Empire in Asia, 1500–1700: A Political and Economic History* (New York: Longman Publishing, 1993), 30.

[6]Diffie and Winius, *Foundations*, 14.

[7]M. N. Pearson, *The Portuguese in India*, The New Cambridge History of India (Cambridge: Cambridge University Press, 1987), 18–19.

[8]Diffie and Winius, *Foundations*, 18.

[9]Subrahmanyam, *The Portuguese Empire*, 33.

[10]Ibid., 43.

[11]Pearson, *The Portuguese in India*, 15.

[12]Penelope Carson, "Christianity, Colonialism, and Hinduism in Kerala: Integration, Adaptation, or Confrontation?" in *Christians and Missionaries in India: Cross-Cultural Communication since 1500*, ed. Robert Eric Frykenberg (Grand Rapids, MI: Eerdmans, 2003), 135.

[13]Subrahmanyam, *The Portuguese Empire*, 38.

[14]Pearson, *The Portuguese in India*, 16.

[15]Subrahmanyam, *The Portuguese Empire*, 49.

[16]Jaison Mulerikkal, "Early Masses in Malabar: The St. Thomas Christians of India," November 19, 2009, http://asiapacific.anu.edu.au/blogs/southasiamasala/2009/11/19/early-masses-in-malabar-the-st-thomas-christians-of-india/.

[17]Placid Podipara, *The Malabar Christians* (Alleppey, India: Prakasam Publications, 1972), 27.

[18]The apocryphal *Acts of Thomas* is the work most often cited for this tradition. See A. F. J. Klijn, *The Acts of Thomas: Introduction, Text, Commentary*, Supplements to Novum Testamentum 5 (Leiden: E. J. Brill, 1962).

[19]Eusebius of Caesarea, *Historia Ecclesiastica*, trans. Gustave Bardy (Paris: Éditions du Cerf, 1955), 2:39–40.

[20]Leonard Fernando and G. Gispert-Sauch, *Christianity in India: Two Thousand Years of Faith* (New Delhi: Penguin Books India, 2004), 59.

[21]The Thomas Christians of southern India are not the only communities that claim a connection to St. Thomas. Other Thomite communities were established in Persia and Syria. See Joseph Kallarangatt, "St. Thomas Christians of India: Ecclesiological Heritages and Perspectives before the 17th Century," *Christian Orient* 14, no. 1 (1989): 23–40.

Simplified:

[1]Bailey W. Diffie and George D. Winius, *Foundations of the Portuguese Empire 1415–1580*, Vol. I, Europe and the World in the Age of Expansion. Minneapolis: University of Minnesota Press, 1977, 181.

[2]For more on the Jesuits in India, see Teutonio R. de Souza and Charles J. Borges, eds., *Jesuits in India: In Historical Perspective*. Goa: Xavier Center of Historical Research, 1992.

[3]Paulo da Trindade, *Conquista Espiritual do Oriente*, ed. Felix Lopes. Lisbon: Centro de Estudos Historicos Ultramarinos, 1962, 82.

[4]Diffie and Winius, *Foundations*, 9.

[5]Sanjay Subrahmanyam, *The Portuguese Empire in Asia, 1500–1700: A Political and Economic History*. New York: Longman Publishing, 1993, 30.

[6]Diffie and Winius, *Foundations*, 14.

[7]M. N. Pearson, *The Portuguese in India*, The New Cambridge History of India. Cambridge: Cambridge University Press, 1987, 18–19.

[8]Diffie and Winius, *Foundations*, 18.

[9]Subrahmanyam, *The Portuguese Empire*, 33.

[10]Subrahmanyam, 33.

[11]Pearson, *The Portuguese in India*, 15.

[12]Penelope Carson, "Christianity, Colonialism, and Hinduism in Kerala: Integration, Adaptation, or Confrontation?" in Robert Eric Frykenberg, ed., *Christians and Missionaries in India: Cross-Cultural Communication since 1500*. Grand Rapids, MI: Eerdmans, 2003, 135.

[13]Subrahmanyam, *The Portuguese Empire*, 38.

[14]Pearson, *The Portuguese in India*, 16.

[15]Subrahmanyam, *The Portuguese Empire*, 49.

[16]Jaison Mulerikkal, "Early Masses in Malabar: The St. Thomas Christians of India," November 19, 2009. Online at asiapacific.anu.edu.

[17]Placid Podipara, *The Malabar Christians*. Alleppey, India: Prakasam Publications, 1972, 27.

[18]The apocryphal *Acts of Thomas* is the work most often cited for this tradition. See A. F. J. Klijn, *The Acts of Thomas: Introduction, Text, Commentary*, in Vol. V, Supplements to Novum Testamentum. Leiden: E. J. Brill, 1962.

[19]Eusebius of Caesarea, *Historia Ecclesiastica V,* in Gustave Bardy, translator, *Eusèbe de Cesarée, Histoire Ecclesiastique,* book II. Paris: Éditions du Cerf, 1955, 39–40.

[20]Leonard Fernando and G. Gispert-Sauch, *Christianity in India: Two Thousand Years of Faith.* New Delhi: Penguin Books India, 2004, 59.

[21]The Thomas Christians of southern India are not the only communities that claim a connection to St. Thomas. Other Thomite communities were established in Persia and Syria. See Joseph Kallarangatt, "St. Thomas Christians of India: Ecclesiological Heritages and Perspectives before the 17th Century," *Christian Orient* 14:1 (1989), 23–40.

Sample Bibliography

This bibliography cites the same works as the endnotes listed above. Note the features of the bibliography: works are alphabetized by author's surname, each work appears only once, and there are no numbers preceding the listings in the bibliography. Page numbers are included only for the articles and for chapters in books, not for books themselves. Even if you have used footnotes and included all of the information in those footnotes, you will still need a bibliography. Notice too that all works used in the preparation of the paper are listed in the bibliography, even if they were not specifically cited in the footnotes.

Chicago:

Carson, Penelope. "Christianity, Colonialism, and Hinduism in Kerala: Integration, Adaptation, or Confrontation?" in *Christians and Missionaries in India: Cross-Cultural Communication since 1500,* edited by Robert Eric Frykenberg, 127–54. Grand Rapids, MI: Eerdmans, 2003.

Da Trindade, Paulo, *Conquista Espiritual do Oriente.* Edited by Felix Lopes. Lisbon: Centro de Estudos Historicos Ultramarinos, 1962.

De Souza, Teutonio R., and Charles J. Borges, eds. *Jesuits in India: In Historical Perspective.* Goa: Xavier Center of Historical Research, 1992.

Diffie, Bailey W., and George D. Winius. *Foundations of the Portuguese Empire 1415–1580*. Europe and the World in the Age of Expansion 1. Minneapolis: University of Minnesota Press, 1977.

Eusebius of Caesarea. *Historia Ecclesiastica*. Translated by Gustave Bardy. Paris: Éditions du Cerf, 1955.

Fernando, Leonard, and G. Gispert-Sauch. *Christianity in India: Two Thousand Years of Faith*. New Delhi: Penguin Books India, 2004.

Kallarangatt, Joseph. "St. Thomas Christians of India: Ecclesiological Heritages and Perspectives before the 17th Century." *Christian Orient* 14, no. 1 (1989): 23–40.

Mulerikkal, Jaison. "Early Masses in Malabar: The St. Thomas Christians of India." November 19, 2009. Http://asiapacific. anu.edu.au/blogs/southasiamasala/2009/11/19/early-masses-in-malabar-the-st-thomas-christians-of-india/.

Pearson, M. N. *The Portuguese in India*. The New Cambridge History of India. Cambridge: Cambridge University Press, 1987.

Podipara, Placid. *The Malabar Christians*. Alleppey, India: Prakasam Publications, 1972.

Subrahmanyam, Sanjay. *The Portuguese Empire in Asia, 1500–1700: A Political and Economic History*. New York: Longman Publishing, 1993.

Simplified:

Carson, Penelope, "Christianity, Colonialism, and Hinduism in Kerala: Integration, Adaptation, or Confrontation?" in Robert Eric Frykenberg, ed., *Christians and Missionaries in India: Cross-Cultural Communication since 1500*. Grand Rapids, MI: Eerdmans, 2003, 127–154.

Da Trindade, Paulo, *Conquista Espiritual do Oriente*, ed. Felix Lopes. Lisbon: Centro de Estudos Historicos Ultramarinos, 1962.

De Souza, Teutonio R., and Charles J. Borges, eds., *Jesuits in India: In Historical Perspective*. Goa: Xavier Center of Historical Research, 1992.

Diffie, Bailey W., and George D. Winius, *Foundations of the Portuguese Empire 1415–1580*, Vol I, Europe and the World in the Age of Expansion. Minneapolis: University of Minnesota Press, 1977.

Eusebius of Caesarea, *Historia Ecclesiastica V,* in Gustave Bardy, trans., *Eusèbe de Cesarée, Histoire Ecclesiastique,* book II. Paris: Éditions du Cerf, 1955.

Fernando, Leonard, and G. Gispert-Sauch, *Christianity in India: Two Thousand Years of Faith.* New Delhi: Penguin Books India, 2004.

Kallarangatt, Joseph, "St. Thomas Christians of India: Ecclesiological Heritages and Perspectives before the 17th Century," *Christian Orient* vol. 14, no. 1 (1989), 23–40.

Mulerikkal, Jaison, "Early Masses in Malabar: The St. Thomas Christians of India," November 19, 2009. Online at asiapacific. anu.edu.

Pearson, M. N., *The Portuguese in India,* The New Cambridge History of India. Cambridge: Cambridge University Press, 1987.

Podipara, Placid, *The Malabar Christians.* Alleppey, India: Prakasam Publications, 1972.

Subrahmanyam, Sanjay, *The Portuguese Empire in Asia, 1500–1700: A Political and Economic History.* New York: Longman Publishing, 1993.

The Author-Date System of Documentation

The author-date system of documentation uses in-text citation instead of footnotes and a "works cited" page instead of a bibliography. This method is seldom used within the study of religion, with few publications employing it, as the study of religion generally demands more information than this method provides. Use this method of citation only if your professor accepts it. Again, be clear about citation requirements for that particular class before you put a lot of effort into the paper. The discussion of the author-date system follows Chicago style throughout.

In-Text Citation

In-text citation means that the citation for the material you are using or quoting from is incorporated into the running text instead of being placed in a note. The name of the author, the date the source was published, and the page number are enclosed in parentheses at the end of the sentence, with complete information detailed at the end of the paper. Use an in-text citation anywhere a footnote would otherwise be needed.

This method makes no distinction between authors and editors or between different types of materials for in-text citation. Use the name of the person who will be listed first on the works-cited page as the name in the citation in your text. Again, a college library or writing center should be able to help you with this citation method.

Basic Citation

If you are not identifying the author in the body of the sentence, include the author's name, the year of publication, and the number of the page where the quotation is found in parentheses after the end of the sentence.

> Another definition of sin is "the failure to bother to love" (Keenan 2004, 55).

If you have identified the author in the body of the sentence, include only the year of publication and the page number of the work in parentheses following either the author's name or the quotation, as in these examples:

> James Keenan argues that sin may be seen as "the failure to bother to love" (2004, 55).

or

> James Keenan (2004, 55) argues that sin may be seen as "the failure to bother to love."

Authors with Similar Names

When citing works by two different authors with the same surname, distinguish the authors by using the first initial of the first name along with the surname.

> (R. Niebuhr 1956, 61)

> (H. Niebuhr 1951, 22)

Multiple Authors

When a work has two authors, use both names in the in-text citation:

(Barsotti and Johnston 2004, 99)

When a work has three or more authors, use the name of the first named author and the phrase *et al.* to indicate that several people were involved in the composition of the work.

(Ring et al. 1998, 44)

Works Cited

The author-date system links the in-text citations with a "works cited" page, which gives details for all of the materials cited in the paper. Every citation within the text must have a corresponding entry on the works cited page. Without this entry, a reader has no details or information about the materials used in the paper. Place the list of works cited at the end of the paper. Begin on a new piece of paper, not on the bottom of the last page of your paper.

Every item *cited* in the paper has an entry on the works cited page, not every item *consulted*. If you have consulted a number of works that helped you form opinions about your paper topic but have not cited those works in your paper, consider using a "works consulted" page instead. This lists all of the materials consulted for the paper, not only those cited.

Whether you choose to list everything cited or everything consulted, list your sources in detail in alphabetical order by the author's surname. Works listed on the "works cited" page follow the same format as a bibliography except that the date is placed immediately after the name or names of the author or authors:

Barsotti, Catherine M., and Robert K. Johnston. 2004. *Finding God in the Movies: 33 Films of Reel Faith.* Grand Rapids, MI: Baker Books.

5

A BRIEF REVIEW OF ENGLISH GRAMMAR

The word *grammar* refers to the basic structure and rules of language. Most of these conventions are learned through everyday use. Written grammar has some rules that are different from spoken grammar. The more writing (and reading) you do, the better your writing will become. Through practice and exposure, you will quickly learn to incorporate the rules of written grammar into your work.

Knowing the rules of grammar has another use within the study of religion or theology, especially for more advanced work in these fields. Written texts are important for many religious traditions, and most of these texts are not written in English. Understanding English grammar—the parts of speech, the structure of sentences and clauses, and the use of words—will make learning the languages of scriptures easier. Translation will be easier, and the mechanics of language and translation styles will make more sense the more you understand about English.

BASIC GRAMMAR

Grammar Checkers: A Warning

Most commercially available word processing programs include a grammar checker, and many others are available online. Grammar checkers are fairly useless when it comes to writing well, and they will distract you from focusing on your topic. Grammar checkers frequently miss grammar errors and suggest incorrect substitutions. Language and meaning are complex and cannot be seriously evaluated by a machine. This is especially true when writing about religion, which is subject to interpretation and emotion. Do yourself a favor by turning off the grammar checker and learning the rules of language so that you can evaluate your own writing.

Sentences

Sentences are a basic unit of written communication. There are four basic types: declarative, imperative, interrogative, and exclamatory. A declarative sentence makes a statement or tells a fact. An imperative sentence issues a command or request. An interrogative sentence asks a question and usually ends with a question mark. An exclamatory sentence expresses surprise or strong emotion and usually ends with an exclamation point. The vast majority of your work will be written in declarative sentences.

Examples:

Declarative: The Bible is a book by many authors.

Imperative: Bring your papers to class on Thursday.

Interrogative: Who wrote the Bible?

Exclamatory: Theology is the most exciting subject!

When writing, it is important to construct complete sentences, avoiding both sentence fragments and run-on or sprawling sentences. The following examples illustrate some of the differences.

This is an example of a complete sentence, with a subject, verb, and object:

Religion classes require good writing.

In this example, *religion classes* is the subject, *require* is the verb, and *writing* is the object. This is a complete sentence. (Please note, however, that a sentence does not need an object to be complete. For example, "Jesus wept" and "God exists" are complete sentences.)

This example includes an incomplete sentence:

Writing well in religion classes. Good writing can help your grade.

In this example, the first phrase, *writing well in religion classes*, ends with a period as though it were a complete sentence. *Writing well in religion classes* is a sentence fragment, however, because it lacks a verb and an object and does not express a complete thought. This is an example of a run-on sentence:

> Religion classes require good writing, attendance, and group projects and they also may require some research or other big papers, including research papers and presentation papers, along with attention to details and reading homework for every class.

Although it is a complete sentence, it can easily be broken into three separate sentences:

> Religion classes require reading, writing, attendance, and group projects. In writing, religion classes may require research papers, presentation papers, and other big papers. Whether in reading or writing, attention to detail is important.

Subject-Verb Agreement

If the subject of a sentence is singular (refers to one person, place, object, or idea), the verb used in that sentence should also be singular. Plural subjects require plural verbs.

Examples:

The students study together on Tuesdays.

The student studies in the library on Tuesdays.

Clauses

Simple sentences have single subjects, verbs, and objects. There is nothing wrong with simple sentences that quickly convey a thought or other information. More complex sentences may join several clauses. You may find it helpful to identify different types of clauses in determining the punctuation for the sentence.

An independent clause has a subject and a verb and could stand alone as a complete sentence. Independent clauses are joined to make compound sentences, often by using a conjunction like *and*, *but*, or *yet*.

Example:

Confucianism is most often practiced in China, but it is also practiced in countries with large Chinese populations.

A dependent clause standing alone would be an incomplete sentence or a sentence fragment. Dependent clauses do not express a complete thought but join with independent clauses to form complex sentences. Dependent and independent clauses are joined with coordinating conjunctions (and, but, or) or with a subordinating conjunction (although, because, unless).

Example:

We plan to go to the beach tomorrow, unless it rains.

Nouns and Pronouns

A noun is a person, place, or thing. Religious ideas, concepts, buildings, congregations and people are all nouns. Common nouns refer to general objects, people, or ideas. Proper nouns refer to specific people, places, or things. An example of a common noun would be *weekday*; a corresponding proper noun would be *Tuesday*. Names of people, places, religions, sacred texts, colleges and universities, and other institutions are all proper nouns. See below for the capitalization of common and proper nouns.

Collective nouns are singular nouns that refer to groups of things: a pride of lions, a herd of cows, a gaggle of geese. Collective nouns have singular verbs and objects.

Pronouns are words that stand in for or take the place of nouns. Pronouns can be general (both, each, their, we) or gender-specific (he, his, her, she). Pronouns should agree in number with the nouns they replace. That is, a singular pronoun should replace a singular noun and a plural pronoun should replace a plural noun.

For information on using pronouns in regard to deities or revered persons, see chapters 2 and 3.

Adjectives and Adverbs

Adjectives and adverbs are modifiers. They add details or somehow modify, or change, nouns and verbs. Adjectives describe or modify nouns. An adjective will usually tell a reader the quality of a thing (that is a *beautiful* butterfly), how many of a thing (*several* books are on the shelf), or indicate which one (*these* activities are boring). Adjectives are usually placed before the nouns they modify.

Proper adjectives are those that are derived from proper nouns. For example, *Chinese* is a proper adjective when used in phrases like *the Chinese people*. Proper adjectives are capitalized.

Adverbs describe or modify verbs and can also modify adjectives or other parts of a sentence. Many people recognize adverbs by the suffix *–ly*, though not all adverbs have this construction. Adverbs usually tell how something is done (slowly or quickly), or when (after, during, while). Adverbs can be used in many parts of a sentence.

Plurals

Plurals indicate that there is more than one of something. In English, simple plurals are formed by adding *-s* to the ends of nouns:

books, desks, pens, computers

If a noun ends in *s, z, x, ch,* or *sh,* form a plural by adding *–es*:

beaches, foxes, dashes

If a noun ends in *y,* drop the *y* and add *–ies*:

families, babies, puppies

If a noun ends in *o,* it may form a plural by adding either *–s* or *–es,* depending on the word:

potatoes, autos

There are also many irregular plural forms in English. For example, the plural of man is men, the plural of child is children, and the plural of deer is deer. The only thing to do about irregular plurals is to memorize them or look them up.

▶ Remember that subjects and verbs must agree: singular subject-singular verb, plural subject-plural verb. ◀

Possessives

Although they also often end in *s*, possessives are different from plurals. Possessives indicate ownership in a linguistic sense. Although plurals are formed by adding –*s*, possessives are formed by adding an apostrophe with an –*s*.

To form a singular possessive, add an apostrophe and an –*s* to the end of a word:

Lonergan's ideas

the professor's notes

the student's computer

If a singular noun ends in *s*, there are two options. One is to add an apostrophe and an -*s* as with singular possessives. The other is to add just the apostrophe. The important thing is to be clear that the noun is still singular. Choose the method that seems clearest to you and makes the most sense in your paper and be consistent with it.

Sykes's teachings or Sykes' teachings

To form plural possessives, first form the plural and then add the apostrophe. For plural nouns that end in –*s*, add just an apostrophe to form a plural possessive:

students' grades

professors' meetings

For plural nouns that don't end in –*s*, add an apostrophe and an –*s* to form a plural possessive.

people's time

children's books

For compound subjects, it matters whether ownership is singular or plural. If ownership is singular, use the possessive only on the last noun:

Steven, Bob, and Terri's presentation

If the ownership is plural, use a possessive on each noun:

Steven's, Bob's, and Terri's presentations

Capitalization

Proper capitalization makes writing easy to read and understand. Use a capital letter to start a sentence, for the personal pronoun I, for the first word and other important words in a title, and for the names of days of the week, months, and holidays.

Capital letters are also used for proper names. A person's name is always capitalized, no matter where it appears in a sentence. Names of specific places, such as cities, states, and countries, are also capitalized.

People's titles are capitalized only when they are attached to their names. Otherwise they are common nouns and are not capitalized. For example:

Pope John Paul II, the pope

Archbishop Desmond Tutu, the archbishop

Metropolitan Alexis IV, the metropolitan

President Barack Obama, the president

The names of religions are proper nouns and are capitalized, as are any modifiers formed using those terms. The terms for people who follow that religion are also capitalized. For example:

Christianity, Christian, Methodists, Baptists

Sikhism, Sikh

Islam, Muslims

The names of deities or revered persons in religions are proper nouns and, therefore, are always capitalized.

God, Jesus, Allah, Moses, Muhammad, Christ, Krishna, Rama, Buddha

▶ Random capitalization can be very distracting and detract from your writing. When in doubt, use the lowercase. ◄

Names

Respecting human beings means using their names properly. Make sure all of the names in your paper are spelled correctly, the way that the person prefers. When in doubt, check the name in your source material.

Within your paper, when referring to a person for the first time, use the person's full name and his or her title, if appropriate. Every time you refer to the same person after that, use only the person's surname. This may seem awkward at first, but it makes papers easier to read.

First reference:	Every other reference:
Fr. Joseph Sullivan	Sullivan
Archbishop David Shannon	Shannon, or the archbishop
Karl Rahner, SJ	Rahner
Dr. Cecilia Moore	Moore

When two people in your paper have the same surname, use their first names with their surnames throughout the paper for clarity.

Dealing with Numbers

Spell out the numbers from one through ten and use numerals for any numbers larger than that. Always spell out a number that begins a sentence.

three, six, 432, 906

Forty years after the war,

Eleven million people

Use numerals for all dates, but spell out the names of months. Use a comma between the date and the year.

July 4, 1776

August 16, 1958

To indicate a time span in years, use a hyphen between the two years.

1445-1463

1963-1971

Never begin a sentence with a year. Rewrite your sentence so that the year does not come first.

Not this: 1789 was the beginning of the French Revolution.

Use this instead: The French Revolution began in 1789.

USAGE

Usage refers to the way words are used and the use of the proper word to convey the author's intended meaning. Using the wrong word or using a word improperly can change the meaning of a sentence or an argument. Usage errors most often occur when words are used similarly but mean different things. If you are unsure of a word, look up its definition to be certain that you are using it correctly.

What follows are some common usage errors. Many others are listed online and in good style books. Be sure to use these words correctly. Also see the section on homonyms in chapter 6 and the section on religious usage in chapter 1.

in actual fact
Use *in fact* instead.

affect, effect
Affect is a verb that means "to influence"; *effect* is a noun that means "outcome" and a verb that means "to bring about."

based off of
Use *basis* or *based on* instead.

definitely, defiantly
Definitely means "certainly"; *defiantly* mean "rebelliously."

due to the fact of
Use *because* instead.

former, latter
The former is the first of two things, the latter is the second.

irregardless
This is an improper form of the word *regardless*. Use *regardless* instead.

its, it's

Its is the possessive form of *it*; *it's* is the contraction for *it is*.

less, fewer

Use *less* with singular nouns and *fewer* with plural nouns.

penultimate

This means next to last, not something beyond ultimate.

principle, principal

A principle is a rule of some type; a principal is a person in authority, a loan amount, or a primary role.

prophesy, prophecy

Prophesy is the verb; *prophecy* is the noun.

tenet, tenant

A tenet is a principle or a belief; a tenant is a person who rents space from a landlord.

there, their, they're

There indicates a place, *their* is a possessive pronoun, and *they're* is the contraction for they are.

upmost, utmost

The correct word is *utmost*. *Upmost* is not generally accepted as a word.

very unique

Something that is unique is one of a kind. Something cannot be very unique.

who, whom

Whom is not a better-sounding or more formal form of *who*. Do not just replace *who* with *whom*. *Who* is a subject; *whom* is an object.

who's, whose

Who's is a contraction of *who is*; *whose* is a possessive.

your, you're

Your is the possessive of *you*; *you're* is the contraction for *you are*.

6

THE BASICS
OF PUNCTUATION

Correct punctuation is essential to any written work. The rules of punctuation are all about clear and effective communication, and learning these rules will make writing easier and more satisfying.

Although punctuation has many rules, exceptions to those rules are plentiful, as well. If you are unsure about punctuation, consult a modern style guide. Several are listed in appendix B, "Helpful Resources," that should be available in your college library.

Italics

Although it is proper to use italics for the titles of long or permanent works, such as books, journals, magazines, websites (but not pages or articles within websites), movies, musical compositions, and works of art such as paintings and sculptures, the title of any scriptural work is treated differently. Capitalize but do not italicize scriptural works such as Bible, New Testament, Tanak, Torah, Qur'an, and Upanishads.

Italicize words in foreign languages unless they are common or are in a foreign typeface, like Greek or Hebrew. In most cases, Spanish words that are commonly used in the United States, like "casa" and "padre," do not need to be italicized.

Italics can also be used to emphasize a word or phrase, but use this technique sparingly or it will become ineffective or even annoy readers.

Periods

Periods end most declarative and imperative sentences.

Periods are placed inside parentheses when the material in parentheses is a complete sentence. A period in a quotation also goes before, not after, the closing quotation mark.

Ellipses

An ellipsis is a series of three periods in succession. An ellipsis is usually used in formal writing to indicate that something has been left out of a direct quotation or that something is missing in the text. Very long quotations with many dependent clauses can be shortened to the essentials by using an ellipsis in place of nonessential information in the quote. Do not use an ellipsis in other ways in your paper.

▶ Be careful not to change the meaning of a quotation when shortening it using an ellipsis. Don't change an author's writing to fit your own meaning. For example, note the difference in meaning when ellipses replace words in the following quote:

"The movie was a tremendous waste of time and money!"

"The movie was . . . tremendous . . . !"

Be especially thoughtful when shortening quotations from religious works, many of which have subtle nuances and shades of meaning. ◄

Commas

Commas are used to indicate any break in a sentence, usually separating two clauses within the same sentence. Commas can also be used to separate some elements of a sentence, such as descriptive phrases, adjectives, and introductory words or phrases.

Use a comma:

After most introductory phrases and some introductory words:

However, not all Buddhists practice the same kinds of meditation.

In addition, Bonhoeffer became an opponent of many church leaders.

Before and after descriptive or parenthetical phrases:

> Krishna and Arjuna, both revered in the Hindu tradition, are the main characters in this writing.

> Most Christians believe that baptism, a sacred rite, is essential for believers.

Before conjunctions that join independent clauses:

> The choir did not have much time to practice, but the music during the service was lovely.

To set off nonrestrictive words, phrases, or clauses:

> Pope Leo X, one of the Medici popes, was one of Raphael's most important patrons.

> Confucius, whose work became widespread after his death, believed that people could learn how to build great societies.

Do not use commas:

To separate the subject and verb:

Incorrect:

> Bernard Lonergan, was an important theologian in the twentieth century.

Correct:

> Bernard Lonergan was an important theologian in the twentieth century.

Between the verb and the object:

Incorrect:

> The author of the book spoke, to the class.

Correct:

> The author of the book spoke to the class.

Between parallel elements:

Incorrect:

> Peace, and nonviolence are important to the Jains.
>
> The Buddha was inspired by the suffering he saw, and by his own experiences.

Correct:

> Peace and nonviolence are important to the Jains.
>
> The Buddha was inspired by the suffering he saw and by his own experiences.

Items in a Series

Use commas to separate items in a series. Use a comma after each item in the series, including the one before the conjunction.

> Three of the most important gods of the Hindu tradition are Brahma, Shiva, and Vishnu.

Semicolons

Use a semicolon to separate items in a series when those items have other punctuation associated with them.

> Three of the most important gods of the Hindu tradition are Brahma, who is the creator and has the responsibility of forming new souls; Shiva, the transformer or destroyer, who is often depicted as a many-limbed dancer; and Vishnu, the preserver of all things who has many popular avatars.

Semicolons are used to join two independent clauses without a conjunction. This indicates that the two clauses are closely related.

> Theological study requires curiosity and attention to detail; creativity and imagination are also useful in approaching this topic.

▶ If you are unsure whether to use a semicolon or a comma, try simplifying the sentence, possibly rewriting it as two sentences so that you are sure of the punctuation. It's better to have a simpler sentence that is easily understood than a complex sentence that makes no sense. ◄

Colons

Colons can separate two independent clauses, especially when the first clause introduces the second clause or the second amplifies or restates the point of the first.

Colons can also introduce lists that are not preceded by a verb, a preposition, or word such as *namely*. You would write "The study explored three religions: Hinduism, Sikhism, and Islam," but "The study explored Hinduism, Sikhism, and Islam," and "The study explored three religions, namely, Hinduism, Sikhism, and Islam." Colons may also be used when quotations are introduced with *thus* or *the following*. For example, "Robert Bellah wrote the following: . . ."

▶ If you are unsure of whether to use a colon, comma, or period to introduce a quotation, consult your professor or teaching assistant or a style guide such as *The Chicago Manual of Style*. ◄

Question Marks

Question marks indicate direct questions and end interrogative sentences. Few question marks should appear in formal papers, except in direct quotations.

Question marks go inside quotation marks when the quotation is a question and outside quotation marks when the entire sentence that includes the quotation is a question. For example:

Did she say, "My foot hurts"?

She asked, "Does your foot hurt?"

▶ Rhetorical questions are questions that are asked to make a point and for which no answer is expected. Limit the use of rhetorical questions in your papers. They serve little purpose and are often a substitute for critical thinking. Instead, provide enough information to answer anticipated questions about your work. ◄

Exclamation Points

Exclamation points mark the end of most exclamatory sentences and indicate emphasis, irony, surprise, or other strong emotions. Exclamation points should generally be avoided in formal papers, except in direct quotations.

Hyphens, Dashes, and Slashes

Hyphens are used in several ways. Hyphens separate some compound words and names and are also used to separate numbers and letters in some sequences, such as phone numbers and email addresses.

Use a hyphen in compound adjectives, to join equal nouns, and for clarity after some prefixes.

a scholar-athlete

Dashes are slightly longer than hyphens and have different uses. Dashes are used to replace some other punctuation, such as commas or parentheses, usually for emphasis. They can also be used in place of ellipses in some cases to indicate that material is missing or has been omitted for another reason.

The Confucian canon—especially the Analects—has been important in the development of Chinese society.

Slashes are most often used in Internet addresses but have few other uses in formal writing. They are used to indicate a choice between equivalents, such as and/or, East/West, red/green. See the section on inclusive language in chapter 1 for the use of the construction his/her.

Slashes are also commonly used to indicate *per*, as in $5/hour. In formal writing, however, spell out the words you mean instead of using slashes: $5 per hour.

Parentheses and Brackets

Parentheses enclose material that is not essential to the sentence but is included to explain or expand on the information in the sentence. Use parentheses around sentence fragments that would interrupt the original sentence but still provide information related to the sentence.

▶ If you find that you want to enclose more than a sentence fragment in parentheses, either rewrite the sentence or put some of your material in an explanatory footnote. ◄

Parentheses are also used to enclose translated or transliterated words within a sentence.

The biblical book John contains many *ego eimi* (I am) statements.

Brackets [ ] (sometimes called square brackets) are not interchangeable with parentheses. Brackets are used inside parentheses to avoid having double or triple parentheses. Brackets can also sometimes be used to indicate material missing from sacred manuscripts and other texts.

If square brackets are included in a text that you are quoting, be sure to include the brackets with the quotation even if parentheses would be correct.

Quotation Marks

Quotation marks are used to denote any material that is a direct quotation from another source and around titles of articles and other works.

There are several ways to incorporate a quotation into your work. One way is the partial quotation, where a part of a sentence or a phrase from another author becomes a part of your own sentence. The words that are not your own are enclosed in quotation marks. For example:

Lebret believed that poverty and hunger constitute "the tragedy of the century."[4]

or

"The tragedy of the century," according to Lebret, consists of poverty and hunger.[5]

Another way to use quotations is to use a complete sentence from the text, set off by quotation marks. For example:

Lebret said, "Endless poverty and the hunger that afflicts so many is the tragedy of the century."[6]

Notice the punctuation in the sentences above. Periods and other final punctuation go inside the quotation marks. The footnote number is placed outside the quotation marks and is not followed by any other punctuation.

For quotations longer than three sentences or about 100 words, do not use quotation marks but rather set the quote apart from the text by using double indention and single spacing. This is called a block quotation. Use block quotations when a short quotation will not properly convey the original author's meaning.

Special Characters

Ampersand (&)

Do not use an ampersand (&) to mean *and* in any formal writing. Use it only if it appears in a direct quotation.

Braces { }

Braces (sometimes called curly braces or curly brackets) are not interchangeable with parentheses. Generally these will not be used in papers about religion.

Mathematical Characters

There may be a few times when you need to used some kinds of formulas or mathematical constructs in your papers. Keep these to a minimum and copy them exactly into your paper.

Money ($)

Use the dollar sign ($) instead of spelling out *dollars*. So: $5 million, not 5 million dollars.

Bulleted Lists

Bulleted lists can be useful, but keep them short. For a bulleted list longer than five items, consider whether you could convey this information in a better way.

Words as Words

When using a word as a word, italicize it for clarity.

The word *regardless* is often misused.

Foreign Languages

Writing about religion often means doing research or using materials in foreign languages. This is especially true in advanced classes in biblical studies and some classes in world religions. Materials in other languages can strengthen research papers if they are used properly.

The main requirement for working with a foreign language is that you understand the language and make a sincere attempt to understand the point the author is trying to make. Regardless of your proficiency, keep a dictionary and grammar handy, as theological writing in any language can contain many unfamiliar words and constructions.

Italicize foreign words in your paper unless they are in a script other than English, such as Greek, Hebrew, or Hindi. Make sure that you preserve all of the correct punctuation, vowel points, and accent marks in your text, as the meanings of some words change depending on where some marks are placed. As noted above, commonly used words, such as "adios," "avatar," and "padre," do not need to be italicized.

Unless your paper is a word study, avoid using single words and very short phrases in foreign languages when the same meaning can be communicated in English. For longer quotations, provide an English translation, either within your text or in a footnote, and indicate whether this is your own translation or from another source.

As always, do not include in your writing anything you do not understand.

Punctuation Involving the Internet

Assignments for class are mostly formal writing, while much of the writing on the Internet is informal, sometimes very informal. Don't mix the elements of informal writing with the more formal writing required for class. This means that most abbreviations, especially acronyms like LOL, should be avoided in papers. Similarly, emoticons have no place in class papers.

Internet addresses include long strings of numbers, letters, and symbols. Avoid these whenever possible, but if you must have a long string of letters and numbers in a paper or a reference, don't add to or subtract anything from it. Don't add hyphens, even when the address will be split at the end of a line. Don't add periods to the address, either, even if adding a period will split the address across lines in a more logical way or preserve the formatting at the end of a page.

When submitting your paper in print, make sure to remove all of the hyperlinks that will print in another color.

Because it is a proper noun, the word *Internet* is always capitalized.

Spelling Checkers

Even in this age of computerized spelling checkers, correct spelling is the responsibility of the student. Spelling checkers can tell only if you have spelled a word correctly, not if you have used it properly. For example, you may type the word *profit*, which is correctly spelled but incorrectly used if you are writing about the prophets of the Hebrew scriptures. Similarly, a spell checker would find nothing wrong with the *Ten Comments*, even if what you meant to type was *Ten Commandments*. Only a human being can determine which words and phrases are correct.

Additionally, many words used in the study of religion are not included in the spelling checkers most commonly in use. You will have to verify the spelling of theological words on your own. Names, especially names associated with world religions, are also not included in most spelling programs. Use dictionaries or theological works to check the spelling of theological or religious words and names. When you have a choice between correct spellings, use the most common, which is usually listed first.

British English

Some students have become enamored of the British spellings of common English words, substituting *colour* for *color* and *realise* for *realize*, for example. Unless you were raised in the United Kingdom or Canada and learned to read and write there, use the standard American spellings for words, except in direct quotations. The same is true for British idioms and other words with different American definitions, such as substituting the word *lorry* for *truck*. Use common American English instead.

If you are from the United Kingdom or Canada, use an American spell-checking program and a good American dictionary to check your papers.

Use of *sic*

Sometimes there are spelling or other errors in published works, or there are words or phrases in older works that are not used in the same way as they are today. If you are using a quotation that has such an error and you cannot avoid using the portion with the error, add the word *sic* in brackets after the word to indicate that the error is in the original and is not your mistake. Notice that the word is italicized, because it is a Latin term. For example:

"The reciept [*sic*] of the Bible in that area was very enthusiastic."

Homonyms

One of the major sources of spelling errors in papers is homonyms, words that sound alike when spoken but have different meanings and different spellings. *Profit* and *prophet* are examples of this. Spelling and grammar programs will not catch these errors. Below is a partial list of homonyms to use carefully.

aid, aide	know, no
altar, alter	meat, meet
bean, been	one, won
bear, bare	passed, past
bloc, block	peace, piece
born, borne	Pilate, pilot
brake, break	pray, prey
buy, by, bye	profit, prophet
canon, cannon	right, rite, write
cast, caste	sole, soul
cite, site, sight	there, their, they're
do, due	threw, through
hi, high	to, too, two
him, hymn	vary, very
it's, its	weather, whether
knew, new	who's, whose

PAPER-WRITING CHECKLIST AND FORMATTING TIPS

PAPER-WRITING CHECKLIST

Before submitting your paper, review this list to be sure that you have turned in the best possible work that accurately reflects your time and effort. As always, check to be sure that you have met all of your instructor's directions as well as these more general guidelines. For help with any area of this checklist, see the chapters indicated.

- Is this paper or assignment interesting and well organized? Would you want to read it if you did not have to? (*chapter 1*)
- Does this paper or assignment meet the criteria outlined in the assignment? Is it the right type of paper for that assignment? (*chapter 1*)
- If your paper is a research paper, does it have a clearly articulated thesis statement and a well-reasoned argument with supporting evidence? (*chapter 1*)
- Are all of your sentences complete thoughts, without sentence fragments or run-on sentences? (*chapter 5*)
- Have you cited your sources properly? (*chapter 4*)
- Is your usage correct? Are you sure? (*chapters 5 and 6*)
- Is everything spelled correctly? Have you checked the spelling yourself to make sure that the spell-checking program caught all the errors and did not insert others? (*chapters 5 and 6*)
- Have you checked your punctuation? (*chapter 6*)

- Is the paper properly formatted? (*section below and your professor's instructions*)
- Is your name on the paper's cover page, first page, or every page, depending on the type of paper and your professor's preferences? (*section below*)

And most important . . .

- Does this paper reflect your best work?

FORMATTING TIPS

If your professor gives you formatting instructions, follow them. If not, the following general guidelines will help ensure a good-looking, easy-to-read paper.

- Always type your papers. Many professors won't accept anything handwritten.
- Use black ink on white paper.
- Use a 12-point font for your paper's running text (see below for more on fonts).
- For footnotes or endnotes, use the same typeface as is used in the running text. It is usually acceptable to use a 10-point size for notes.
- Double-space the text in your papers.
- Use margins no bigger than 1 inch all around. Don't dishonor yourself by trying to lengthen your paper artificially by using larger margins.
- Number your pages, using plain numerals, not Roman numerals or anything stylized.
- Use a cover page for research papers, but most other papers will not require a cover page. Don't use sheet protectors or other types of covers for your paper. For most instructors, all that is required is a staple to hold the pages together. Ask your instructor if you are unsure of this or any other instruction.

- On the cover sheet for a research paper, type the title of your paper, your name, and any other information required, such as date, name of course, and name of instructor.
- If you use your professor's name on your paper, be sure to spell it correctly.

Fonts

Today's word processing programs make it easy to change the size and style of type and to add decorative elements to a paper. In general, avoid all of this in any formal writing for a class. As beautiful as a "designed" paper may look to you, it may also distract from the ideas in the paper. Choose a typeface that is easy to read and set that typeface as a default to use in all of your class assignments. Keep the size used for the running text consistent throughout your paper. A simple, easy-to-read design will let your ideas shine through.

The exceptions to this are the few times when you may want to use Hebrew or Greek characters for advanced papers in biblical studies classes. In that case, be very careful to copy the Hebrew or Greek characters exactly, including any accents or other pronunciation marks. Do not use these characters if you do not understand them or are unsure of how to use them properly. Never use Hebrew or Greek characters as mere decorations in a paper.

▶ Some word processing programs allow students to choose a size between 12 and 13 points, such as 12.3 or 12.5. Don't do this in your papers. Professors can tell when the sizes have been manipulated in order to make a paper appear longer. ◄

HELPFUL RESOURCES

This appendix provides a list of resources that will provide more information on the issues discussed in this book. Most of these are useful for both professors and students, although some of the style guides may focus on issues that are too complex or involved for people who do not work with religious texts and writing every day. Most of these resources were consulted in the writing of this book.

Alexander, Patrick H., ed. *The SBL Handbook of Style: For Ancient Near Eastern, Biblical, and Early Christian Studies.* Peabody, MA: Hendrickson Publishing, 1999. Online at *www.sbl-site. org/publications.* A PDF download designed especially for students is also available at *www.sbl-site.org/assets/pdfs/sblhs_ss92804_ revised_ed.pdf.*

This is a guide to citation and usage of ancient Jewish and Christian texts, including the Bible and materials related to it. This book may be in your college library, but you will likely find the PDF summary worksheet more useful.

Bowker, John, ed. *The Oxford Dictionary of World Religions.* New York: Oxford University Press, 2006.

This work provides good information on the basic beliefs, deities, and rituals associated with many world religions. A copy can usually be found in your college library.

Catholic News Service. *CNS Stylebook on Religion: Reference Guide and Usage Manual.* 3rd ed. Washington, DC: Catholic News Service, 2006.

This is a stylebook for the Catholic News Service, showing usage for many words associated with Catholicism. It also contains helpful lists of abbreviations for religious orders and other groups associated with the Roman Catholic Church.

The Chicago Manual of Style: The Essential Guide for Writers, Editors, and Publishers. 16th ed. Chicago: University of Chicago Press, 2010. Available online at *www.chicagomanualofstyle.org.* A very helpful quick citation guide is also available at *www.chicago manualofstyle.org/tools_citationguide.html.*

This book offers a guide to all things associated with citation and usage. It also includes some information on writing techniques. The book should be available in your college library, and many summary sheets are available online, from your library, or from the college writing center.

DeSena, Laura Hennessey. *Preventing Plagiarism: Tips and Techniques.* Urbana, IL: National Council of Teachers of English, 2007.

This is a practical guide for teachers and professors, including how to shape assignments to prevent plagiarism among students.

Garner, Bryan A. *Garner's Modern American Usage.* 3rd ed. New York: Oxford University Press USA, 2009.

This work is a helpful guide to using words and language to communicate effectively. It includes guides to words that have developed new meanings and words that may be offensive.

Gilmore, Barry. *Plagiarism: A How-Not-To Guide for Students.* Portsmouth, NH: Heinemann, 2009.

This is a detailed student guide to avoiding plagiarism, including instructions on when footnotes are needed and how to use paraphrasing properly.

Hudson, Robert. *The Christian Writer's Manual of Style.* Grand Rapids, MI: Zondervan, 2006. Also available as an e-book.

This work provides a guide to using words properly, especially as they relate to religion. It also includes helpful sections on avoiding problematic words, using inclusive language, and the proper spelling and usage of words from major world religions.

Maggio, Rosalie. *Talking about People: A Guide to Fair and Accurate Language.* Phoenix: Oryx Press, 1997.

This book provides a guide to using words in reference to people and avoiding offense.

MLA Handbook for Writers of Research Papers. 7th ed. New York: Modern Language Association of America, 2009.

The style handbook of the Modern Language Association, this work includes information on usage and citation, using an in-text format. The official online guide requires a subscription, but style sheets are available many places online or through your college library or writing center, which should also have a copy of this book.

Nichols, Larry A., George Mather, and Alvin J. Schmidt. *Encyclopedic Dictionary of Cults, Sects, and World Religions.* Rev. and updated ed. Grand Rapids, MI: Zondervan, 2006.

This book offers a guide to the origin and practice of many different religious groups.

O'Conner, Patricia T. *Woe Is I: The Grammarphobe's Guide to Better English in Plain English.* 3rd ed. New York: Riverhead Books, 2009.

This is a guide to English grammar. Look here for information on sentences, sentence structure, and general writing information.

Snow, Kathie. "To Ensure Freedom, Inclusion, and Respect for All, It's Time to Embrace People-First Language." *Disability Is Natural,* 2010. Online at *www.disabilityisnatural.com.*

This work provides a style guide for people-first language.

Strunk, William, Jr., and E. B. White. *The Elements of Style.* 4th ed. Boston: Allyn and Bacon, 2000.

This is the classic guide to good writing. It is likely to be in your college library or writing center.

Truss, Lynne. *Eats, Shoots & Leaves.* New York: Gotham, 2004.

This book offers an entertaining guide to English grammar that addresses common mistakes.

Turabian, Kate L., et al. *A Manual for Writers of Research Papers, Theses, and Dissertations: Chicago Style for Students and Researchers.* 7th ed. Chicago: University of Chicago Press, 2007.

This book provides a user-friendly guide to issues about writing, especially Chicago-style citation. It is likely to be in your college library or writing center.

Zinsser, William. *On Writing Well: The Classic Guide to Writing Non-Fiction.* 7th ed. New York: HarperCollins, 2006.

This guide to good writing is likely to be in every college library or writing center.

Index